All in one Word Processing

Sr. Maddy Takyala

(Sr. Magdalene Claire Takyala Nakimbugwe)

ISBN-10 : **1724238337**
ISBN-13: 978-1724238337

ABOUT THE BOOK

This book moves the user step by step in to using Microsoft word, excel, access, PowerPoint. It's a very useful resource for business professionals, graphic designers and anyone who wants to do creative and professional writing.

CONTENTS

x

Preface

Is this book relevant to you? In these pages , I explain step by step how to use Microsoft word, Access, excel and PowerPoint.

For those who have not yet been familiar with the use of the Microsoft software, this book will take you step by step into getting acquainted with the terms and how to write professionally. I describe the overall use of the mircosoft software and lead readers to additional rescouces where they can find additional information.

My goal is to give you the reader the ability to practice and apply Microsoft tools, commands so that to make their work look not only professional but creative.

ACKNOWLEDGEMENTS

I am very grateful to my family, friends, and my congregation for all the prayers, love and support.

CHAPTER 1

1.1 Word processing keyboard shortcuts

It's very important to know the shortcuts to save time when using word processing. There are shortcuts with Word Shortcut Key Combinations with CTRL + "A-Z", Word Shortcut Key Combinations with CTRL + SHIFT + "A-Z" , Word Shortcut Key Combinations with CTRL + ALT + "A-Z", and Word Shortcut Key Combinations" with CTRL + "Special Keys"

Short Cut	Meaning
Ctrl + A	Select all text in Word Document
Ctrl + B	Bold the selected Text
Ctrl + C	Copy the selected text
Ctrl + D	Open font formatting window
Ctrl + E	Center text
Ctrl + F	Find a word or phrase
Ctrl + G	Go to specific page or bookmark
Ctrl + H	Find and Replace a word or phrase
Ctrl + I	Italicize the text
Ctrl + J	Justify the text
Ctrl + K	Opens "Insert Hyperlink" window
Ctrl + L	Left align text
Ctrl + M	Indent a paragraph from the left
Ctrl + N	Open a new MS Word Document
Ctrl + O	Open an existing MS Word Document
Ctrl + P	Print the document
Ctrl + Q	Remove paragraph formatting
Ctrl + R	Right align text
Ctrl + S	Save MS Word document
Ctrl + T	Create a hanging indent
Ctrl + U	Underline selected text

Ctrl + V	Paste copied text
Ctrl + W	Close Word Document
Ctrl + X	Cut selected text
Ctrl + Y	Redo an action previously undone or repeat an action
Ctrl + Z	Undo a previous action
Ctrl + Shift + C	Copy formats
Ctrl + Shift + D	Double underline text
Ctrl + Shift + E	Track changes
Ctrl + Shift + F	Change the font
Ctrl + Shift + H	Apply hidden text formatting
Ctrl + Shift + K	Format letters as small capitals
Ctrl + Shift + L	Apply the list style
Ctrl + Shift + M	Remove the paragraph indent from the left
Ctrl + Shift + N	Apply the normal style
Ctrl + Shift + P	Change the font size
Ctrl + Shift + Q	Change the selection to Symbolic font
Ctrl + Shift + S	Apply a style
Ctrl + Shift + T	Reduce a hanging indent
Ctrl + Shift + V	Paste formats
Ctrl + Shift + W	Underline words but not spaces
Ctrl + Shift + >	Increase font size
Ctrl + Shift + <	Decrease font size
Ctrl + Alt + I	Switch in or out of print preview
Ctrl + Alt + M	Insert a comment
Ctrl + Alt + R	Insert Registered trademark symbol
Ctrl + Alt + S	Insert copyright symbol
Ctrl + Alt + T	Insert trademark symbol
Ctrl + [	Decrease size of selected text
Ctrl +]	Increase size of selected text
Ctrl + 1	Single space lines
Ctrl + 2	Double space line

Ctrl + 5 1.5	space lines	
Ctrl + Left Arrow	Move one word to the left	
Ctrl + Right Arrow	Move one word to the right	
Ctrl + Up Arrow	Move one paragraph up	
Ctrl + Down Arrow	Move one paragraph down	
Ctrl + Page Up	Go to the top of previous page	
Ctrl + Page Down	Go to the top of next page	
Ctrl + END	Go to the end of the document	
Ctrl + Home	Go to the beginning of the document	
Ctrl + Enter	Page break	
Ctrl + Delete	Delete one word to the right	
Ctrl + Backspace	Delete one word to the left	
Ctrl + TAB	Insert a "TAB" character	

1.2   What is word processing.

A word processor is an electronic device or computer application software that perform word processing: the composition, editing, formatting and sometimes printing.

of any sort of written material. Word processing can also refer to advanced shorthand techniques, sometimes used in specialized contexts with a specially modified typewriter. The term was coined at IBM's Böblingen, West Germany Laboratory in the 1960s. Typical features of a word processor include font application, spell checking, grammar checking, a built-in thesaurus, automatic text correction, Web integration and HTML exporting, among others.

The word processor emerged as a stand-alone office machine in the 1970s and 1980s, combining the keyboard text-entry and printing functions of an electric typewriter with a dedicated computer processor for the editing of text. Although features and designs varied among manufacturers and models, and new features were added as technology advanced, word processors typically featured a monochrome display and the ability to save documents on memory cards or diskettes. Later models introduced innovations such as spell-checking program Microsoft, improved formatting options, and dot-matrix printing As the more versatile combination of personal computers and printers became commonplace, and computer software applications for word processing became popular, most business machine companies stopped manufacturing word processor machines. As of 2009 there were only two U.S. companies, Classic and Alpha Smart, which still made them. Many older machines, however, remain in use. Since 2009, Sentinel has offered a machine described as a "word processor", but it is more accurately a highly specialized microcomputer used for accounting and publishing. Word processors are descended from early text formatting tools (sometimes called "text justification" tools, from their only real capability). Word processing was one of the earliest applications for the personal computer in office productivity.

Word processing

Word processing is an application program that allows someone to create letters, reports, newsletters, tables, form letters, brochures, and Web pages. Using this application program someone can add pictures, tables, and charts to the documents. Someone can also check spelling and grammar.

OTHER WORD PROCESSING APPLICATIONS

- WordPerfect (which
- Microsoft's MICROSOFT-DOS operating system) and open source applications OpenOffice.org
- Writer
- LibreOffice Writer
- AbiWord,KWord,
- LyX. Web-based word processors,such as Office Web Apps or Google Docs, are a relatively new category.

Main features of word processing applications:

- Work on multiple documents simultaneously

- With the help of mail merge, someone can quickly create merge documents like

mass mailings or mailing labels
- Create professional documents fast, using built-in and custom templates
- Easily manage large documents using various features like the ability to create

table of contents, index, and cross-references
- Work on multiple documents simultaneously
- With the help of mail merge, someone can quickly create merge documents like

mass mailings or mailing labels
- AutoCorrect and AutoFormat features catch typographical errors automatically

and allow someone to use predefined shortcuts and typing patterns to quickly format the documents.

- The print zoom facility scales a document on different paper sizes, and allows someone to print out multiple pages on a single sheet of paper.
- The nested tables feature supports putting one table inside another table.
- Export and save the word documents in PDF and XPS file format.
- Batch mailings using form letter template and an address database (also called mail merging);
- Indices of keywords and their page numbers;
- Cross-referencing with section or page numbers.
- Tables of contents with section titles and their page numbers;
- Tables of figures with caption titles and their page numbers;

Footnote numbering;

- New versions of a document using variables (e.g. model numbers, product names, etc.)
- Other word processing functions include spell checking (checks against wordlists), "grammar checking" (checks for what seem to be simple grammar errors), and a "thesaurus" function (finds words with similar or opposite meanings). Other common features include collaborative editing, comments and annotations, support for images and diagraMicrosoft and internal cross-referencing.

Almost all word processors enable users to employ styles, which are used to automate consistent formatting of text body, titles, subtitles, highlighted text, and so on. Word processing greatly simplify managing the formatting of large documents, since changing a style automatically changes all text that the style has been applied to. Even in shorter documents styles can save a lot of time while formatting. However, most help files refer to styles as an 'advanced feature' of the word processor, which often discourages users from using styles regularly.

1.3 New features of 2016 word

MICROSOFT Word 2016 has useful features and tools introduced to produce professionally created documents.

Someone can easily create, format, edit professional-looking user

document using comprehensive set of easy to use tools provided by MICROSOFT Word. It uses the MICROSOFT Office Fluent user Interface concept. This interface uses a new component called Ribbon to group the tools by task, within task by sub tasks and related commands that are used more frequently. The new user results oriented interface

presents the tools to someone in a more organized and efficient manner, which are easy to locate.

1. Tabs are more task oriented such as Home, Insert, Page

2. Within each tab, the related sub-tasks are grouped together

3. Related command buttons are also grouped together to execute a command

or to display a command menu.

Importance of Microsoft word

➢ Microsoft Office Word 2016 helps someone produce professional-looking documents by providing a comprehensive set of tools for creating and formatting the document in a new interface. Rich review, commenting, and comparison capabilities help someone quickly gather and manage feedback from colleagues. Advanced data integration ensures that documents stay connected to important sources of business information.

➢ The Microsoft Word 2016 provides a lot of pre-formatted template to produce documents, reports etc. While using the pre-formatted template, someone can select already available cover page, header and footer to give the documents a professional look without spending much time in formatting a new one.

➢ Microsoft Word 2016 also provides features for creating chart and diagram which include three-dimensional shapes, transparency, drop shadows, and other effects. This helps create highly professional documents with flexibility in representing data more efficiently and professionally.

➢ Before sharing a document, which is in its final form with others, someone can use MICROSOFT Word 2016 "Mark As Final" features to protect the document from any changes. "Mark as Final" command makes the document "read-only" making the typing, editing and proofing command disabled.

➢ MICROSOFT Word 2016 also provides the feature and tools to export the document to either PDF (Portable Document Format) or XPS (XML Paper Specification) format.

➢ Create professional-looking documents Office Word 2016 provides editing and reviewing tools for creating polished documents more easily than ever before.

➢ Microsoft word presents tools to someone when someone need them, in a clear and organized fashion.

➢ Save time and get more out of the powerful Word capabilities by selecting from galleries of predefined styles, table formats, list formats, graphical effects, and more. Microsoft Word helps in formatting the document. The galleries of formatting choices give someone a live visual preview of the formatting in the document before someone commit to making a change.

➢ Microsoft office Word introduces building blocks for adding preformatted content to the documents: For example, when someone is working on a document from a template type, such as a report, someone can select from a gallery of preformatted cover pages, pull quotes, and headers and footers to make the document look more polished.

➢ In case someone want to customize the preformatted content, or if the organization often uses the same piece of content, such as legal disclaimer text or customer contact information, someone can create the own building blocks that someone select from the gallery with a single click.

➢ Word processing allows the user to Communicate more effectively with high-impact graphics due to the new charting and diagramming features include three-dimensional shapes, transparency, drop shadows, and other effects.

➢ Word helps one to Instantly apply a new look and feel to the documents when the company updates its look, someone can instantly follow suit in the documents.

➢ Using word makes it possible to use Quick Styles and Document Themes, someone can quickly change the appearance of text, tables, and graphics throughout the document to match the preferred style or color scheme.

➢ With Microsoft word it's Easy to avoid spelling errors due to the spelling checkers.
The spelling checker has been made more consistent across the 2016. The spelling checker can find and flag some contextual spelling errors. someone can type a mistake similar to the following? I will see someone there. In Office Word 2016, someone can enable the Use contextual spelling option to get help with finding and fixing this type of mistake. This option is available when checking the spelling of documents in English, German or Spanish.

➢ The 2016 Microsoft Office system spelling checker includes the post-reform French

dictionary. In Microsoft Office 2003, this was an add-in that had to be
separately installed. For more information, see Change the way spelling and
grammar checking work.

➢ For those who want to learn more vocabulary. An exclusion dictionary is automatically created for a language the first time that language is used. Exclusion dictionaries let someone force the spelling checker flag words someone want to avoid using. They are handy for avoiding words that are obscene or that don't match the style guide. For more information, see Use exclusion dictionaries to specify a preferred spelling for a word.

➤ Word helps one to Share documents confidently. When someone send a draft of a document to the colleagues for their input, Office Word 2016 helps someone efficiently collect and manage their revisions and comments. When someone is ready to publish the document, Office Word 2016 helps someone ensure that any unresolved revisions and comments aren't still lurking in the published document.

➤ Word helps one to quickly compare two versions of a document Office Word 2016 makes it easy to find out what changes were made to a document. When someone compare and combine documents, someone can see both versions of the document — with the deleted, inserted, and moved text clearly marked in a third version of the document.

➤ Word helps one to find and remove hidden metadata and personal information in documents. Before someone share the document with other people, someone can use the Document Inspector to check the document for hidden metadata, personal information, or content that may be stored in the document. The Document Inspector can find and remove information like comments, versions, tracked changes, ink annotations, document properties, document management server information, hidden text, custom XML data, and information in headers and footers. The Document Inspector can help someone ensure that the documents someone share with other

people do not contain any hidden personal information or any hidden content that the

➤ organization might not want distributed. Additionally, the organization can customize the Document Inspector to add checks for additional types of hidden content.

➤ Word allows one to even add a digital signature or signature line to the documents. Someone can help provide assurance as to the authenticity, integrity, and origin of the document by adding a digital signature to the document. In Office Word 2016 someone can either add an invisible digital signature to a document, or someone can insert a

Microsoft Office Signature Line to capture a visible representation of a signature along with a digital signature.

➢ Also, the ability to capture digital signatures by using signature lines in Office documents makes it possible for organizations to use paperless signing processes for documents like contracts or other agreements. Unlike signatures on paper, digital signatures provide a record of exactly what was signed, and they allow the signature to be verified in the future.

➢ Office Word 2016 supports exporting the file to the following formats:

• **Portable Document Format (PDF)** PDF is a fixed electronic file format that preserves document formatting and enables file sharing. The PDF format ensures that when the file is viewed online or printed, it retains exactly the
 format that someone intended, and that data in the file cannot be easily changed. The PDF format is also useful for documents that will be reproduced by using commercial printing methods.

• **XML Paper Specification (XPS)** XPS is an electronic file format that
preserves document formatting and enables file sharing. The XPS format
ensures that when the file is viewed online or printed, it retains exactly the
format that someone intended, and that data in the file cannot be easily changed.

➢ Word makes it possible to Instantly detect documents that contain embedded macros. Office Word 2016 uses a separate file format (.docm) for macro-enabled documents, so someone can instantly tell whether a file can run any embedded macros.

➢ Word prevents changes to a final version of a document before someone share a final version of a document with other people, someone can use a Mark As Final command to make the document read-only and communicate to other people that someone are sharing a final version of the document. When a document is marked as final, typing, editing commands, and proofing marks are disabled, and people who view the document cannot inadvertently change the document. The **Mark as Final** command is not a security feature. Anyone can edit a document that is marked as final by turning off **Mark as Final**.

➤ Microsoft Word goes beyond documents because now more than ever, when computers and files are interconnected, it pays to store documents in files that are slim, sturdy, and supportive of a wide variety of platform Microsoft.

To meet this need, the Microsoft Office system achieves a new stage in its evolution of XML support. The new XML-based file format enables Office Word 2016 files to be smaller, more robust, and deeply integrated with information internal and external data sources.

➤ Word also reduces file sizes and improve corruption recovery. The new Word XML format is a compressed, segmented file format that offers a dramatic reduction in file size and helps ensure that damaged or corrupted files can be easily recovered.

➤ Word processing helps to Connect the documents to business information.

In the business, someone create documents to communicate important business data. Someone can save time and reduce the risk of error by automating the process of this communication. Create dynamic smart documents using new document controls and data binding to connect to the back-end.

➤ Microsoft also Manage document properties in the Document Information Panel.

The Document Information Panel makes it easy to view and edit document properties while someone work on the Word document. The Document Information Panel displays at the top of the document in Word. Someone can use the Document Information Panel to view and edit both standard Microsoft Office document properties and properties for files that are saved to a document management server. If someone use the Document Information Panel to edit the document properties for a server document, the updated properties will be saved directly to the server. For example, someone may have a server that keeps track of a document's editorial status. When someone put the finishing touches on a document, someone can open the Document Information Panel to change the document's editorial status from Draft to Final. When someone save the document back on the server, the change in editorial status is updated on the server.

➢ If someone store document templates in a library on a Microsoft Windows SharePoint Services 3.0 server, the library might include custom properties that store information about the templates. For example, the organization may require someone to categorize documents in the library by filling in a Category property. Using the Document Information Panel, someone can edit properties like this directly within the Word environment.

➢ **Recover from computer problems with** 2016 Microsoft Office system provides improved tools for recovering the work in the event of a problem in Office Word 2016.

➢ **Office Diagnostics:** Microsoft Office Diagnostics is a series of diagnostic tests that can help someone to discover why the computer is crashing. The diagnostic tests can solve some Microsoft problems directly. Microsoft Office Diagnostics replaces the following Microsoft Office 2003 features: Detect and Repair and Microsoft Office Application Recovery.

➢ Word has Program Recovery In particular Office Word 2016 has improved capabilities

to help avoid losing work when the program closes abnormally. Whenever possible, Word tries to recover some aspects of the state of the program after it restarts. For example, someone is working on several files at the same time. Each file is open in a different window with specific data visible in each window. Word crashes. When someone restart Word, it opens the files and restores the windows to the way they were before Word crashed.

1.4 Word Processing Basics

The word screens

The Word screen (Window) contains many objects such as Tabs, Menus, Sub menus, short-cut commands etc.

Menus: If someone are familiar with previous versions of Word, when someone begin to explore Word 2016, someone will notice a significant change in the menu structure, look and feel.

The features in Word 2016 display as various tabs such as Home, Insert, Page layout References, Mailings, Review and View etc.

To view all sub tasks/options (expanded form) in each menu, someone must click the required option. For example, the images below show the Border menu in collapsed form and in expanded form as shown in the pictures below.

Shortcut Menus: These features allow someone to access various Word commands faster than using the options on the menu bar. When the menu is expanded, the shortcut menu is displayed with short-cut command option for each of the short-cut menu item.

The options on this menu will vary depending on the sub-task that was clicked or selected. For example, the shortcut menu on the side is produced by selecting or expanding the Border option of the paragraph sub-task of the Home Tab from the Tab bar. The shortcut menus are helpful because they display only those options that can be applied to the item that was selected and, therefore, prevent searching through the many menu options.

TOOL BARS USED IN MICROSOFT-WORD

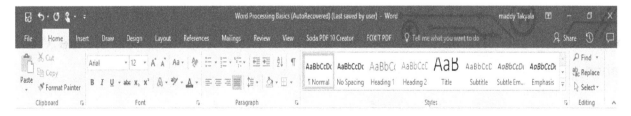

MICROSOFT Word 2016 provides a customized quick access toolbar to organize the tools available for easy and fast access of the commands. Many toolbars displaying shortcut buttons are also available to make editing and formatting quicker and easier.

The toolbars that are already displayed on the screen are checked. To add/modify simply click on the "More Commands" option which will display the following menu for customized selection of tools as per the requirement.

Rulers:

The rulers display horizontal and vertical scales that reflect the width and height of the typing area. The horizontal scale is invaluable when someone want to quickly set tabs, margins, and indents. Select the View tab on the main MICROSOFT word 2016 screen to be able to select/deselect the Ruler/Gridlines and other options.

Vertical and Horizontal Scrollbars:

The typing area is bordered on the right side by the vertical scroll bar with a scroll button and arrows. The single down arrow scrolls through the document line by line. The double down arrow allows someone to move to the top of the next page. The double up arrow allows someone to move to the top of the previous page. The double down arrow allows someone to move to the top of the next page. Someone can also drag the vertical scroll button up and down the scroll bar to move up and down through the document.

The first bar along the bottom of the typing area is the horizontal scroll bar. To see the text that is off the right side of the screen, use the left arrow button. To see the text that is off the left side of the screen, use the right arrow button. Someone can also drag the horizontal scroll button to move left or right of the document. In Word 2016, the options

such as view documents and zoom are also available on the bottom bar for easy access.

1.5 USING THE HELP FUNCTION IN MICROSOFT-WORD

Microsoft Word has its own built-in help system. This can be accessed by clicking on the [Help] button on the far right of the Word window (just under the x to close Word). If someone get used to using help then someone should be able to solve the Microsoft problems. To demonstrate how the system works, look up how to make the text bold:

1. Click on the [Help] button – a Word Help window appears

2. Type the word bold into the Search help box and press <Enter> - a list of topics

should appear

3. Click on the topic Make the text bold

The instructions given should be similar to what someone learnt earlier in these notes. Some people like to keep the Word Help window open while they carry out the instructions, but part of the document is covered by the Word Help window. To solve this:

4. At the top of the Word Help window, click on the [Keep On Top] icon

5. This changes to a [Not On Top] icon and now if someone click in the Word document, the Word Help window closes, but is still available as a button on the Taskbar at the bottom of the screen

1.6 SUMMARY

In this chapter, we have discussed about the overview of the Microsoft word. We have discussed about different menus.

Word processing is an application program that allows someone to create letters, reports, newsletters, tables, form letters, brochures, and Web pages. Using this application program someone can add pictures, tables, and charts to the documents. Someone can also check spelling and grammar.

Some of the main features of word processing applications discussed here are:

☐ Create professional documents fast, using built-in and custom templates

☐ Work on multiple documents simultaneously

☐ AutoCorrect and AutoFormat features catch typographical errors automatically and allow someone to use predefined shortcuts and typing patterns to quickly format the documents.

☐ The nested tables feature supports putting one table inside another table.

☐ Batch mailings using form letter template and an address database (also called mail merging);

☐ Tables of contents with section titles and their page numbers;

☐ Cross-referencing with section or page numbers;

☐ New versions of a document using variables (e.g. model numbers, product names, etc.)

MICROSOFT Word 2016 has useful features and tools introduced to produce professionally created documents. Someone can easily create, format, edit professional-looking user document using comprehensive set of easy to use tools provided by MICROSOFT Word. It uses the MICROSOFT Office Fluent user Interface concept. This interface uses a new component called Ribbon to group the tools by task, within task by sub tasks and related commands that are used more frequently. The new user result oriented interface presents the tools to someone in a more organized and efficient manner, which are easy to locate.

1. Tabs are more task oriented such as Home, Insert, Page Layout.

2. Within each tab, the related sub-tasks are grouped together

3. Related command buttons are also grouped together to execute a command

or to display a command menu

We have also discussed about the buttons on the menus in tabular form with them

symbol and description.

Chapter 2

2.1 FORMATTING CHARACTER/ TEXT IN WORD DOCUMENT

Styles

A style is a format enhancing tool that includes font typefaces, font size, effects (bold, italics, underline, etc.), colors and more. Someone will notice that on the Home Tab of the Ribbon, that someone have several areas that will control the style of the document: Font, Paragraph, and Styles.

Change Font Typeface and Size

☐ To change the font typeface:

☐ Click the arrow next to the font name and choose a font.

Remember that someone can preview how the new font will look by highlighting the text, and hovering over the new font typeface.

To change the font size:

☐ Click the arrow next to the font size and choose the appropriate size, or

☐ Click the increase or decrease font size buttons.

Editing Text and Inserting Pictures and WordArt

Font Styles and Effects

Font styles are predefined formatting options that are used to emphasize text. They include: Bold, Italic, and Underline. To add these to text:

☐ Select the text and click the Font Styles included on the Font Group of the Ribbon, or

☐ Select the text and right click to display the font tools

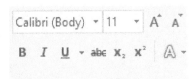

Change Text Color

To change the text color:

☐ Select the text and click the Colors button included on the Font Group of the

Ribbon, or

☐ Highlight the text and right click and choose the colors tool.

☐ Select the color by clicking the down arrow next to the font color button.

Highlight Text

Highlighting text allows someone to use emphasize text as someone would if someone had a marker.

To highlight text:

☐ Select the text

☐ Click the Highlight Button on the Font Group of the Ribbon, or

☐ Select the text and right click and select the highlight tool

☐ To change the color of the highlighter, click on down arrow next to the highlight button.

Copy Formatting

If someone has already formatted text the way someone want it and would like another portion of

the document to have the same formatting, someone can copy the formatting. To copy the formatting, do the following:

☐ Select the text with the formatting someone want to copy.

☐ Copy the format of the text selected by clicking the Format Painter button on the Clipboard Group of the Home Tab

☐ Apply the copied format by selecting the text and clicking on it.

Clear Formatting

To clear text formatting:

☐ Select the text someone wish to clear the formatting

☐ Click the Styles dialogue box on the Styles Group on the Home Tab

☐ Click Clear All

2.2

Editing Text and Inserting Pictures and WordArt

A simple way to select part of the text is by dragging through it as follows:

1. Move the mouse so that the pointer on the screen is at the start of the text that someone want to change.

2. Hold down the mouse button, and keep it held down

3. Drag the mouse sideways to move the pointer to the end of the text that someone would like to change – the selected text now has a blue background

4. When someone is happy with the selection, release the mouse button Someone may have noticed that a set of option buttons have appeared just to the right of the selected text like in the example below:

These different buttons immediately allow someone to change the look of the selected text, eg make it bold, alter the font or size, turn it into a list etc.

If someone accidentally go wrong and select the wrong text, click the mouse once (this will release the selection) and try again.

Tip:

☐ *Minor adjustments to a selected area can be made by holding down the <**Shift**> key and pressing the <**left arrow**> or <**right arrow**> key. This method can also be used instead of dragging through the text. Rows of text can be selected using the <down arrow> or <**up arrow**> keys.*

☐ If ever someone want to replace some words with something different, simply select the words to be replaced and then type the new ones (the selected text automatically disappears). Someone can also delete a section of text by first selecting it and then pressing the <**Backspace**> or <**Delete**> key.

Selecting the Text

Selecting can be done in several different ways, depending on how much text is involved. Any selected text can be de-selected by clicking on the mouse button once.

Try out the following:

☐ **A single word** - point to it using the mouse then double click on the mouse button - the selected word should be highlighted. Click once on the mouse to de-select it.

☐ **A single line** - position the mouse pointer in the left-hand margin (where its shape changes to an arrow pointing inwards) and click once

☐ **A whole paragraph** - either double click in the left margin or click three times within the text

☐ **The whole document** - either click three times in the left margin or press <**Ctrl a**>

☐ **A sentence** - hold down <**Ctrl**> and click anywhere within the sentence

☐ **A short piece of text** - drag through the text to be selected

☐ **A long piece of text** - click at the start of the text to be selected then move down, using the scroll bars, and hold down <**Shift**> as someone click at the end of the selection

☐ **To modify an existing selection** - hold down <Shift> and use the arrow keys

Cut, Copy and Paste

The above buttons are visible on the far left of the **Home** tab in the **Clipboard** group.

Moving text around a document is done by:

☐ Selecting it

☐ Cutting or copying it from its present position

☐ Pasting it back to its new one

Someone can copy information within the same document, from one document to another, or from one program to another (for example, text on a web page can be copied into the Word document).

☐ Move to the top of the document (pressing <**Ctrl Home**> takes someone straight there) and select the first paragraph of text (double click at the left or three times within the paragraph)

☐ Click on the [**Cut**] button and the paragraph will disappear - do not be alarmed,

it has not been lost, but has been copied onto the clipboard

☐ Move the insertion point down to the end of the text (pressing <**Ctrl End**>

moves someone straight there) – add a new line if necessary by pressing <**Enter**>

☐ Click on the [**Paste**] button - the original paragraph will be pasted into its new position

☐ Select the text (or paragraph) whose format someone wish to copy - try the text someone made bold earlier

☐ Click on the [**Format Painter**] button (the pointer becomes a paintbrush)

☐ Drag through another piece of text - release the mouse button and it too becomes bold

This can be especially useful in the case where someone notice that a paragraph looks different from the rest of the paragraphs on that page, maybe because it is in a different font. Someone can use the [**Format Painter**] button to quickly correct this problem.

2.3 Editing Text and Inserting Pictures and WordArt

Making Multiple Copies and the Clipboard

When making multiple copies of text, someone normally **Copy** rather than **Cut** it to the clipboard:

☐ Select some text (a few words will do) and click on the [**Copy**] button (or press <**Ctrl c**> or right click and choose Copy)

☐ The original text will remain where it is, but a copy of it has been placed on the clipboard

☐ Move the insertion point to where someone want to paste the text

☐ Click on the [**Paste**] button (or press <**Ctrl v**> or right click and choose Paste)

☐ Repeat the above step and a second copy of the text will appear

The clipboard, which is normally hidden, will only store the last item that someone cut or copied but, after displaying it, up to 24 items can be stored on it.

To display the clipboard:

☐ Click on the Clipboard group arrow just below the [**Format Painter**] button –

this will open the Office Clipboard in a Task Pane on the left

☐ Select another part of the text and [**Copy**] it - watch it appear on the clipboard

☐ Move the insertion point then click on the new clipboard entry to paste it into the text

☐ Repeat the above step but click on the original clipboard entry

Someone won't need to paste any of the text again, so it's a good idea to empty the clipboard:

☐ Click on the [**Clear All**] button in the Clipboard pane

☐ Close the Task Pane by clicking on its [**Close**] button (the little x in the top right corner)

Drag and Drop

If someone wish to move text a short way then someone can use the drag and drop technique:

☐ Select some text - a few words is sufficient

☐ Move the mouse pointer into the highlighted area then hold down the mouse button (the pointer becomes an arrow with a box attached and in the left-hand corner of the Status Bar at the bottom of the Word window it says Move to where?)

☐ Keeping the mouse button held down, drag the text to a new place in the document (as someone move the cursor a faint dotted line appears - this is where the selected text will be dropped)

☐ Release the button - the text will be moved to its new position

☐ Practice moving selected text to other positions

2.4 FIND, REPLACE AND GO TO FUNCTION

Someone will find the **Find**, **Replace** buttons under the **Editing** group in the **Home** tab, on the extreme **right** side.

Use Microsoft Office Word 2016 to find and replace text, formatting, paragraph

breaks, page breaks, and other Microsoft. Someone can also find and replace noun or adjective for Microsoft or verb tenses.

Someone can extend the search by using wildcards and codes to find words or phrases that contain specific letters or combinations of letters.

Someone can also use the **Go To** command to find a specific place in the document.

Find text

Someone can quickly search for every occurrence of a specific word or phrase.

☐ On the Home tab, in the **Editing** group, click **Find**.

☐ In the **Find what** box, type the text that someone want to search for.

Editing Text and Inserting Pictures and WordArt

Do one of the following:

☐ To find each instance of a word or phrase, click **Find Next**.

☐ To find all instances of a specific word or phrase at one time, click **Find All**,

and then click **Main Document**.

NOTE: *To cancel a search in progress, press ESC.*

Find and replace text

Someone can automatically replace a word or phrase with another — for example, someone can

replace Acme with Apex. The replacement text uses the same capitalization as the text

that it replaces unless someone select the Match case check box. For example, if someone

writes a document with the name Maddy but wants to chance and does not have time to go

through the whole document. She or he will search for Maddy and replace it with Takyala, the

result is Takyala. If the Match case check box is selected, Office Word 2016 searches only for words

that match the case of the word or phrase that someone typed in the Find what box. For

example, if someone search for Maddy , the result includes Maddy but not MADDY.

NOTE: *If someone don't see the Match case check box on the Replace tab, click More.*

☐ On the **Home** tab, in the **Editing** group, click **Replace**.

☐ Click the **Replace** tab.

☐ In the **Find what** box, type the text that someone want to search for.

☐ In the **Replace** with box, type the replacement text.

Do one of the following:

☐ To find the next occurrence of the text, click **Find** Next.

☐ To replace an occurrence of the text, click **Replace**. After someone click **Replace**, Office Word 2016 moves to the next occurrence of the text.

☐ To replace all occurrences of the text, click **Replace All**.

NOTE: *To cancel a replacement in progress, press ESC.*

Go to a specific page, table, or other item

Someone can search for and replace special characters and document elements such as tabs and manual page breaks. For example, someone can find all double paragraph breaks and replace them with single paragraph breaks.

☐ On the **Home** tab, in the **Editing** group, click the **arrow** next to **Find**, and then click **Go To**.

☐ In the **Go to what** box, click the **type** of item.

Do one of the following:

☐ To go to a specific item, type the appropriate identifying information for the item in the Enter item type box, and then click **Go To**.

☐ To go to the next or previous item of the specified type, leave the **Enter box** empty, and then click **Next** or **Previous**.

2.5 SPELLING AND GRAMMAR CHECK

Word checks the spelling and grammar as someone type. A red squiggly line under a word denotes that Word thinks it has been spelt incorrectly; if the line is green then the grammar may be incorrect. Someone can check the whole or part of the text for mistakes using the [Spelling and Grammar] button.

To open the spelling and grammar window:

☐ Click on the **Review** tab

☐ Click on Spelling & Grammar button on the Left side of the tab under the **Proofing** section

☐ Press <**Ctrl End**> to move to the end of the text then <**Enter**> for a new line

☐ Type the following misspelt text:

Note that as someone type the words, Word automatically corrects certain mistakes:

o it capitalizes the first word in a sentence (Howe)

o it corrects certain misspellings (eg studdy to study, garl to girl and sentance to sentence)

☐ Select the line of misspelt text (eg click 3 times on it) - Word can spell-check just a selected area

☐ Move to the Review tab and click on the [Spelling an**d Grammar**] button on the left of the Ribbon

☐ Choose the correct spelling of many in the Suggestions: box – press <**Enter**> for [**Change**]

☐ Continue in the same manner with the other corrections

☐ Always check to make sure it has the correction that you someone want - with and other choose and other If Word gives someone no suggestions (or doesn't show the correct one in the list) someone can edit the text in the Not in Dictionary: box. Also, if a spelling is correct but not in the dictionary, someone can either choose to [**Ignore**] a suggested correction or [**Add**] the word to the own dictionary. Choose [**Ignore All**] if someone don't want to be asked about the same spelling again (similarly [**Change All**] will change all occurrences of a misspelt word). Someone can also [**Close**] or [**Cancel**] the check at any time.

Once the spelling check is complete, the grammar checker is run. This isn't foolproof, but it does pick up some common grammatical mistakes. At the end of the grammar check:

☐ Click on [**No**] - someone don't want the rest of the document checked

☐ Press <**End**> to deselect the highlighted text then <Enter> to start a new paragraph

Tip: If someone just have one word that is misspelt (or a phrase with bad grammar), move the mouse pointer over the error and click on the right mouse button. A list of likely correct spellings appear. If the spelling someone want isn't in the list, choose **Spelling...** **(or Grammar...)** to start the checker.

Note *that someone will still need to proof read the work to pick up, for example, correctly spelt words used in the wrong context. Here, Howe was not corrected because it was recognised as a surname - it would have been picked up had it not been capitalised (by Word itself!). Similarly, on needs manual correction to in. Also, though was was corrected to were in the second sentence, the grammar checker failed to notice that is* *in the first sentence had a plural subject and should be are.*

2.6 AUTOCORRECT FUNCTION

Word's AutoCorrect feature is designed to typos as they occur. Someone've probably noticed that "teh" is changed to "the" and "adn" is changed to "and." This saves someone some time when it comes to editing the document.

AutoCorrect is also used to apply special formatting. For example (c) is changed to the copyright symbol.

Editing Text and Inserting Pictures and WordArt / 41

Like many of Word's features, someone can customize AutoCorrect. Someone can use it to save

some time when someone is working. Someone can assign abbreviations to frequently used names, phrases, and terminology.

To customize AutoCorrect, follow these steps:

☐ From the **File** tab, select Options…

☐ In the **Word Options** window click on the **Proofing button. Proofing** pane will appear

☐ Click on **AutoCorrect Options** Button

In the **Autocorrect** Window

☐ Under **Replace** box type the wrong word that someone always type by mistake.

☐ Under the **With** box type the correct word for the same word.

☐ Click **Add**

☐ Click **OK**

After this, whenever someone type the word that will be replaced with the correct spelling when someone press butto

2.7 WORKING WITH SHAPES, PICTURES, CLIP ARTS AND WORDARTS

The Microsoft Office applications also provide someone with the ability to add a variety of shapes to the Office documents. The Shapes gallery, which someone access via the

Shapes command on the Insert tab, provides many different shape categories.

Someone can add lines, rectangles, block arrows, callouts, and many other different shape types.

One of the available shapes is a text box, which as advertised, is used to add a box containing text to a document. However, other shapes can also contain text; this means that someone can use any shape as a design element and get double duty out of it as a text container. This can be very useful when someone want to add text to a document but also want to add some visual interest at the same time, say in a Word document or a PowerPoint slide. The text in a shape can be formatted using WordArt styles and text fill, outline, and effects tools. This enables someone to create shapes with text entries that are eye-catching and serves an informational purpose in the document.

When someone add a shape to an Office document, the shape is placed on a drawing canvas. This is particularly important in Word and Publisher where a large amount of text might already exist on a page or will exist on the page when the document is complete. The drawing canvas floats on top of the document's text layer. This means that someone don't have to worry about the text layer as someone work with the shapes until someone determine how the shapes will interact with the text in term of the text's alignment with respect to the shape or shapes (which is controlled using the Wrap Text command on the Drawing Tools Format tab).

If someone is working on a flyer or newsletter, WordArt is an effective way to call attention to text. WordArt is text that is formatted to look like a picture. But use WordArt cautiously, or it will make the document appear amateurish.

Graphics can add interest and impact to the Word documents. Suppose someone has completed a letter telling the friends about the great party someone threw for the cat's birthday. The words capture the festive mood of the event, but that page of text books

lifeless and dull. Someone needs graphics to enliven the prose. Photos and other images add visual variety to the Word documents. Someone can use them as decorative features to break up large pieces of text, and they play an important part in delivering the message to the reader. Word offers handy tools for working with images in the documents and, in this article, I'll show someone a few ways to use them.

2.7.1 Adding Shapes

Someone can add one shape to the Microsoft Office 2010 file or combine multiple shapes to make a drawing or a more complex shape. Available shapes include lines, basic geometric shapes, arrows, equation shapes, flowchart shapes, stars, banners, and callouts.

After someone add one or more shapes, someone can add text, bullets, numbering, and Quick Styles to them.

Note For more information about using charts or SmartArt in the document, see When should I use a SmartArt graphic and when should I use a chart?

☐ On the **Insert** tab, in the **Illustrations** group, click **Shapes**.

☐ Click the **shape** that someone want, click anywhere in the document, and then drag to place the shape.

☐ To create a perfect square or circle (or constrain the dimensions of other shapes), press and hold **SHIFT** while someone drag.

Tip: Someone can add individual shapes to a chart or add shapes on top of a SmartArt graphic to customize the chart or SmartArt graphic.

Add multiple shapes to the file

Instead of adding individual shapes to create a drawing, someone might want to create a SmartArt graphic. In a SmartArt graphic, the arrangement of the shapes and the font size in those shapes is updated automatically as someone add or remove shapes and edit the text.

☐ On the Insert tab, in the **Illustrations** group, click Shapes.

☐ Right-click the shape that someone want to add, and then click **Lock Drawing Mode**.

☐ Click anywhere in the document, and then drag to place the shape. Repeat

this for each shape that someone want to add.

Tip: To create a perfect square or circle (or constrain the dimensions of other shapes), press and hold SHIFT while someone drag.

☐ After someone add all the shapes that someone want, press ESC.

Add text to a shape

☐ Click the shape that someone want to add text to, and then type the text.

Notes: *The text that someone add becomes part of the shape — if someone rotate or flip the shape, the text rotates or flips also.*

Add a bulleted or numbered list to a shape

☐ Select the text in the shape that someone want to add bullets or numbering to.

☐ Right-click the selected text, and on the shortcut menu, do one of the following:

☐ To add bullets, point to Bullets, and then choose the options that someone want.

☐ To add numbering, point to Numbering, and then choose the options that someone want.

Add a Quick Style to a shape

Quick Styles are combinations of different formatting options that are displayed in a thumbnail in the Quick Style gallery in the Shape Styles group. When someone rest the pointer over a Quick Style thumbnail, someone can see how the Shape Style (or Quick Style) affects the shape.

☐ Click the shape that someone want to apply a new or different Quick Style to.

☐ Under Drawing Tools, on the Format tab, in the Shape Styles group, click the Quick Style that someone want.

☐ The Format tab under Drawing Tools.

☐ To see more Quick Styles, click the More button.

Change from one shape to another shape

☐ Click the shape that someone want to change to a different shape.

☐ To change multiple shapes, press **CTRL** while someone click the shapes that someone want to change.

☐ Under **Drawing** Tools, on the Format tab, in the Insert **Shapes** group, click Edit **Shape** , point to **Change** Shape, and then click the new shape that someone want.

The shape will get changed in the selected shape. Like shown in the image above the shape will be changed to the cloud shape.

Delete a shape from the file

☐ Click the shape that someone want to delete, and then press **DELETE**.

☐ To delete multiple shapes, press **CTRL** while someone click the shapes that someone want to delete, and then press **DELETE**.

2.7.2 Insert a picture or clip art

Pictures and clip art can be inserted or copied into a document from many different sources, including downloaded from a clip art Web site provider, copied from a Web page, or inserted from a folder where someone save pictures.

Someone can also change how a picture or clip art is positioned with text within a document by using the Position and Wrap Text commands.

Tip: To insert a picture from the scanner or camera, use the software that came with the scanner or camera to transfer the picture to the computer. Save the picture, and then insert it by following the instructions for inserting a picture from a file.

Insert clip art

☐ On the **Insert** tab, in the **Illustrations** group, click **Clip Art**.

Note: Some commands shown are not available in Word Starter.

☐ In the Clip Art task pane, in the Search for text box, type a word or phrase that describes the clip art that someone want, or type in all or some of the file name of the clip art.

To modify the search, do one or both of the following:

☐ To expand the search to include clip art on the Web, click the Include Office.com content checkbox.

☐ To limit the search results to a specific media type, click the arrow in the Results should be box and select the check box next to Illustrations, Photographs, Videos, or Audio.

☐ Click **Go**.

☐ In the list of results, click the clip art to insert it.

☐ To resize clip art, select the clip art someone've inserted in the document. To increase or decrease the size in one or more directions, drag a sizing handle away from or toward the center, while someone do one of the following:

☐ To keep the center of an object in the same location, press and hold CTRL while someone drag the sizing handle.

☐ To maintain the object's proportions, press and hold SHIFT while someone drag the sizing handle.

☐ To both maintain the object's proportions and keep its center in the same location, press and hold both CTRL and SHIFT while someone drag the sizing handle.

Insert a picture from a Web page

☐ Open the document.

☐ From the Web page, drag the picture that someone want into the Word document.

☐ Make sure the picture that someone choose is not a link to another Web page. If someone drag a picture that is linked, it will be inserted in the document as a link instead of an image.

Insert a picture that includes a hyperlink from a Web page

☐ Open the Word document.

☐ On the Web page, right-click the picture someone want, and then click Copy.

☐ In the Word document, right-click where someone want to insert the picture, and then click Paste.

Insert a picture from a file

To insert a picture from the scanner or camera, use the software that came with the scanner or camera to transfer the picture to the computer. Save the picture, and then insert it by following these steps.

☐ Click where someone want to insert the picture in the document.

☐ On the Insert tab, in the Illustrations group, click Picture.

Note: Some commands shown are not available in Word Starter.

☐ Locate the picture that someone want to insert. For example, someone might have a picture file located in **Pictures library**.

☐ Double-click the picture that someone want to insert. Or **Select** the Picture and click **Insert** button

Note: By default, Microsoft Word embeds (embed: To insert information created in one

program, such as a chart or an equation, into another program. After the object is embedded, the information becomes part of the document. Any changes someone make to the object are reflected in the document.) pictures in a document. Someone can reduce the size of a file by linking (link: Used to insert a copy of information created in one program into a Microsoft Word document while maintaining a connection between the two files. When the information changes in the source file, the changes are reflected in the destination documents.) to a picture. In the Insert Picture dialog box, click the arrow next to Insert, and then click Link to File.

☐ To resize a picture, select the picture someone has inserted in the document. To increase or decrease the size in one or more directions, drag a sizing handle away from or toward the center, while someone do one of the following:

☐ To keep the center of an object in the same location, press and hold CTRL while someone drag the sizing handle.

☐ To maintain the object's proportions, press and hold SHIFT while someone drag the sizing handle.

☐ To both maintain the object's proportions and keep its center in the same location, press and hold both CTRL and SHIFT while someone drag the sizing handle

Keep a picture next to the text that goes with it or at a spot on the page

An inline picture keeps its position relative to a portion of the text. Pictures are inserted as inline pictures by default in Word.

A floating picture keeps its position relative to the page, and floats in that position as text flows around it. For example, if someone position the picture halfway down on the left side of the page, and then someone add two paragraphs at the top of the page, the picture will stay halfway down on the left side of the page.

To make sure that the picture stays with text that references it — for example, a

description above the picture, position the picture as an inline picture. If someone add two paragraphs above the description, the picture will move down the page together with the description.

If the picture is not on a drawing canvas (drawing canvas: An area on which someone can draw multiple shapes. Because the shapes are contained within the drawing canvas, they can be moved and resized as a unit.), select the picture. If the picture is on a drawing canvas, select the canvas.

☐ Under **Picture** Tools, on the **Format** tab, in the **Arrange group**, click **Position**.

☐ If someone don't see Position, click **Arrange**, and then click **Position**.

Do one of the following:

☐ To change an inline (inline object: A graphic or another object that is positioned directly in the text of a Microsoft Word document at the insertion point.) picture to a floating (floating object: A graphic or another object that is inserted in the drawing layer so that someone can position it precisely on the page or in front of or behind text or other objects.) picture, select any one of the With Text Wrapping page position options.

☐ To change a floating picture to an inline picture, select In Line with Text.

2.7.3 WordArt

Someone can use WordArt to add special text effects to the document. For example, someone can stretch a title, skew text, make text fit a preset shape, or apply a gradient fill. This WordArt becomes an object that someone can move or position in the document to add decoration or emphasis. Someone can modify or add to the text in an existing WordArt object whenever someone want.

Add a WordArt

☐ On the **Insert** tab, in the **Text** group, click **WordArt**, and then click the **WordArt** style that someone want.

To Modify the WordArt

☐ Select the text to which someone has applied the word art.

☐ Under the **Drawing Tools** tab, go to the **WordArt Style** section.

☐ Open the drop-down list for in built styles

☐ Click on the desired style

Someone can also customize the **WordArt** style by using the options given in the **WordArt Styles** section of **Format** menu of the **Drawing Tools** tab.

Someone can change the color of the WordArt by using **Text Fill** button.

Modify text border using **Text Outline** button.

And give various special effects to the selected WordArt teat like Shadow,

Reflection, 3D Rotation etc. by clicking on the **Text Effects** Button.

When someone remove the WordArt style from the text, the text remains and changes to plain text:

☐ Select the **WordArt** text that someone want to remove the WordArt style from.

☐ Under **Drawing Tools**, on the on the **Format** tab, in the **WordArt Styles**

group, click **Quick Styles** or the **More** button, and then click **Clear**

WordArt.

2.8 SUMMARY

In this chapter we have discussed about text formatting and use of graphics in a word document. Features for working with selected text (Cut, Copy and Paste Functions) and Find, replace and Go To Functions provide the users with a very good level of ease not just to create and edit quality documents but also to navigate through the document in a quick manner.

Spelling and grammar check functionality provides the users with proof-reading benefits. Grammatical and spelling related errors are instantly eliminated through this function. Auto Correct function helps to automatically correct the words in the document. The Shapes, Pictures, Clip Arts and WordArts in MICROSOFT-Word also help the user in creating professional documents in an efficient an quick manner.

In formatting selected text section, we have discussed about selecting, highlighting, coloring, changing font face etc. of selected text.

Selecting text is very important as it identifies which section of text someone want Word to modify. It can be used to change how some text looks, to move or copy text within a document, between documents or between different applications (e.g. Word and PowerPoint), and to delete or replace text.

Someone will find the **Find**, **Replace** buttons under the **Editing** group in the **Home** tab, on the extreme **right** side. Use Microsoft Office Word 2016 to find and replace text, formatting, paragraph breaks, page breaks, and another item. Someone can also find and replace noun or adjective for Microsoft or verb tenses. Someone can extend the search by using wildcards and codes to find words or phrases that contain specific letters or combinations of letters. Someone can also use the **Go To** command to find a specific place in the document.

Word checks the spelling and grammar as someone type. A red squiggly line under a word denotes that Word thinks it has been spelt incorrectly; if the line is green then the grammar may be incorrect. Someone can check the whole or part of the text for mistakes using the [Spelling and Grammar] button.

Like many of Word's features, someone can customize AutoCorrect. Someone can use it to save some time when someone is working. Someone can assign abbreviations to frequently used names, phrases, and terminology.

The Microsoft Office applications also provide someone with the ability to add a variety of shapes to the Office documents. The Shapes gallery, which someone access via the Shapes command on the Insert tab, provides several different shape categories. Someone can add lines, rectangles, block arrows, callouts, and several other different shape types.

If someone working on a flyer or newsletter, WordArt is an effective way to call attention to text. WordArt is text that is formatted to look like a picture. But use WordArt cautiously, or it will make the document appear amateurish.

Graphics can add interest and impact to the Word documents. Suppose someone have completed a letter telling the friends about the great party someone threw for the cat's birthday. The words capture the festive mood of the event, but that page of text looks lifeless and dull. Someone needs graphics to enliven the prose. Photos and other images add visual variety to the Word documents. Someone can use them as decorative features to break up large pieces of text, and they play an important part in delivering the message to the reader.

Chapter 3

3.1 INTRODUCTION

Document management focuses on the storage and organization of documents to support active work in progress, including content creation and sharing within an organization. When organizations do not have any kind of formal document management system in place, content is often created and saved in an unmanaged and decentralized way on scattered file shares and individual hard disk drives. This makes it hard for employees to find, share, and collaborate effectively on content. This also makes it difficult for organizations to use the valuable business information and data in the content.

3.2 WORKING WITH WORD DOCUMENTS

Adding flair to the documents is great, but no one will give someone their business or publish the paper because of the color of the text or the effects on the pie chart. Effective document design is about helping the important information stand out.

Look at two versions of a business letter (In the figure below) to see how basic design elements can make a document more effective.

When someone use a theme in the document, someone automatically get fonts, color, and graphic effects that go together, and someone can format text and graphics with just a few clicks, as someone'll see later in this chapter.

Find many built-in themes in the Themes gallery on the Page Layout tab, in the Themes group, just point to options to preview that theme in the documents.

Someone can also mix and match theme colors, fonts, and effects to quickly create the own look. Select separate theme color, theme font, and theme effect sets from their respective galleries on the Page layout tab.

3.2.1 Add a cover page

Microsoft Word offers a gallery of convenient predesigned cover pages. Choose a cover page and replace the sample text with the own

Cover pages are always inserted at the beginning of a document, regardless of where the cursor appears in the document.

Managing Files

☐ On the **Insert** tab, in the **Pages** group, click **Cover Page**.

☐ Click a cover page Lay out from the gallery of options.

After someone insert a cover page, someone can replace the sample text with the own text by clicking to select an area of the cover page, such as the title, and typing the text.

Notes

☐ If someone insert another cover page in the document, the new cover page will replace the first cover page someone inserted.

☐ To replace a cover page created in an earlier version of Word, someone must delete the first cover page manually, and then add a cover page with a design from the Word gallery.

☐ To delete a cover page inserted with Word, click the **Insert** tab, click **Cover pages** in the **Pages group**, and then click **Remove Current Cover Page**

3.2.2 Apply themes to Word documents

Someone can quickly and easily give the document a professional look by applying a document theme. A document theme is a set of formatting choices that include a set of theme colors, a set of theme fonts (including heading and body text fonts), and a set of theme effects (including lines and fill effects).

Important Document themes that someone apply affect the styles (style: A combination of formatting characteristics, such as font, font size, and indentation store as a set. When someone applies a style, all of the formatting instructions in that style are applied at one time.) that someone can use in the document.

☐ On the **Page Layout** tab, in the **Themes group**, click **Themes**.

☐ Click the document theme that someone want to use.

Notes

☐ If a document theme that someone want to use is not listed, click **Browse for Themes** to find it on the computer or network.

☐ To automatically download new themes, click **Enable Content Updates from Office.com**.

3.2.3 Create document

Getting started with a basic document in Microsoft Office Word 2016 is as easy as opening a new blank document and starting to type.

Or, if someone want to create a specific type of document, such as a business plan or a resumé, someone can save time by starting with a template.

Open a new document and start typing

☐ Click the File tab.

☐ Click New.

☐ Double-click Blank document.

Start a document from a template

The Templates site on Office.com provides templates for many types of documents, including resumés, cover letters, business plans, business cards, and APA-style papers.

☐ Click the File tab.

☐ Click New.

☐ Under Available Templates, do one of the following:

- Click Sample Templates to select a template that is available on the computer.

- Click one of the links under Office.com.

Note: *To download a template that is listed under Office.com, someone must be connected to the Internet.*

☐ Double-click the template that someone want.

Save and reuse templates

If someone make changes to a template that someone downloaded, someone can save it on the computer and use it again. It's easy to find all the customized templates by clicking My templates in the New Document dialog box. To save a template in the My

templates folder, do the following:

☐ Click the **File** tab.

☐ Click **Save As**.

☐ In the **Save As** dialog box, click **Templates**.

☐ In the **Save as type** list, select **Word Template**.

☐ Type a name for the template in the **File name** box, and then click **Save**.

3.2.4 Delete a document

☐ Click the **File** tab.

☐ Click **Open**.

☐ Locate the file that someone want to delete.

☐ **Right-click** the file, and then click **Delete** on the **shortcut** menu.

3.2.5 Saving document

Word's Save As... feature is a great way to save multiple versions of the same file.

Someone can easily preserve earlier versions of the document if someone think someone will need to go back to an earlier stage. One drawback of saving multiple versions of the same file under different names is it can become difficult to manage all the files and it can use a considerable amount of storage space.

To help someone avoid some of these drawbacks while keeping the benefits of preserving drafts of the work, Word includes a Versions feature that allows someone to keep previous versions of the work in the same file as the current document. Someone won't have multiple files, and, since it only saves the differences between the drafts, it saves some of the disk space multiple versions require.

There are two ways to save different versions of the document

1. Someone can save a version manually at any time

2. Or someone can opt to have Word automatically save a version of the document when someone close it

When someone save a file, someone can save it to a folder on the hard disk drive, a network location, CD, DVD, the desktop, flash drive, or in another file format. While someone must identify the target location in the Save in list, the saving process is the same regardless of what location someone choose.

Important: Even if someone has Auto Recover enabled, someone should save the file frequently

while someone is working on it to avoid losing data because of an unexpected power

failure or other problem.

Save a file

By default, the Microsoft Office program saves a file in a default working folder. If someone want, someone can specify a different location.

☐ Click the File tab, and then click Save, or press CTRL+S.

Tip: Click the Save icon on the Quick Access Toolbar.

☐ Someone must enter a name for the file if someone is saving it for the first time.

Save a copy of a file (Save As command)

☐ Click the **File** tab.

☐ Click **Save As**.

☐ Keyboard shortcut: To open the Save As dialog box, **press ALT, F, A**.

☐ In the **File** name box, enter a new name for the file.

☐ Click **Save**.

Tip: *To save the copy in a different folder, click a different drive in the Save in list or a different folder in the folder list. To save the copy in a new folder, click Create New Folder.*

Someone can also use the Save As command to rename a file or change the location of where someone save the file

☐ In the **Save As** window, select the location where someone want to save a copy of file from the location Pane on the left side of Save as window

☐ Someone can rename the file in by changing the **File Name**

Save a file to another format (Save As command)

☐ Click the File tab.

☐ Click Save As.

☐ Keyboard shortcut: To open the Save As dialog box, **press ALT, F, A**.

☐ In the File name box, enter a new name for the file.

☐ In the Save as type list, click the file format that someone want to save the file in. For example, click Rich Text Format (.rtf), Web Page (.htm or .html), or Comma Delimited (.csv).

☐ For more information about how to save files in PDF (.pdf) or XPS (.xps) formats, see Save as PDF or XPS.

☐ Click Save.

Note: *To save to a CD or another location, click the File tab, click Save As, and then click Other Formats. In the Folders list, select a location or the media on which someone want to save.*

Save a file for use in an earlier version of Office

If someone is using Office 2010, someone can save files in an earlier version of Microsoft Office

by selecting the version in the Save as type list in the Save As dialog box. For example, someone can save the Word 2010 document (.docx) as a 97-2003 document (.doc).

Notes

☐ Office 2010 continues the use of the XML-based file formats, such as .docx, .xlsx, and .pptx, introduced in the 2016 Office release. Therefore, files created in Microsoft Word 2010, Microsoft Excel 2010, and Microsoft PowerPoint 2010 can be opened in the 2016 Office release Microsoft without special add-ins or

loss of functionality. For more information, see Open XML Formats and file name extensions.

☐ For more information about compatibility between files from different releases, see Use the Compatibility Checker.

Save Auto Recover information automatically

Auto Recover does not replace regularly saving the files. If someone choose not to save the recovery file after someone open it, the file is deleted, and the unsaved changes are lost. If someone save the recovery file, it replaces the original file, unless someone specify a new file name. The more frequently files are saved, the more information is recovered if there is a power failure or other Microsoft problems while a file is open.

You can also recover by:

☐ Click the File tab.

☐ Under Help, click Options, and then click Save.

☐ Select the Save Auto Recover information every check box.

☐ In the minutes box, type or select a number to determine how often someone want to save files.

3.2.6 Opening document

Someone can open word document two ways:

1. from the **file explorer**. Go to the location where someone has saved the word document. **Double** click on the file. Word document will get opened.

2. Open Microsoft word. Go to **File** menu. Click on **Open** option. The **Open** window will appear on the screen. Go to the file location. Select the file. Click Open button in **Open** window.

☐ Keyboard Short cut for opening the **Open Window: ALT, F, O.**

3.3 WORKING WITH LISTS

Lists are a great way to organize data in documents, and they make it easier for readers to understand key points. Microsoft Word has a tool to create simple

numbered and bulleted lists, and someone can also customize these lists to suit the needs. Here we shall see how to create lists, how to choose the right list for a task, and how to customize them.

Using numbers signifies that the lists are in order or identifies them so they can be referred to more easily.

Why Create Lists?

A list is a good way to organize items in a document because it forces someone to work in a compressed and shortened format, which makes the writing easier to read. Someone can use lists for everything from step-by-step instructions to a series of points that someone want to make and more. When writing step-by-step instructions, be sure to use a verb as the first word in the instructions. This forces someone to be even more succinct.

Use bullet lists when the order of the items in the list doesn't matter. For

example, someone might create a bulleted checklist of items if the actions on the list don't

have to be completed in any particular order. Someone can easily create a checkbox bullet

using a symbol font character.

Where order is critical, such as in step-by-step instructions, use a numbered list rather

than a bulleted list. Numbers reinforce the suggestion that sequence is involved, and

that anyone reading the list should progress from item 1 to item 2 and then 3 and so

on. Numbers are also useful for non-ordered items when someone want to make it easier for

someone to refer to them later on — such as "In reference to item 2..."

How to Create a List

Someone can create a list as someone types it or after someone has finished typing it. To create a list as someone type, click the Numbering or the Bullets button on the Formatting toolbar, and a new number or bullet will appear automatically. Type the first list entry and press Enter to show the next number or bullet. Continue to type the list, and when someone is done, click the Numbering or Bullets icon to turn the feature off.

To create a list after someone have typed the entries, highlight the list and click either the **Numbering** or **Bullets** icon.

Special List Options

When someone need a two-level list, someone can create the second level by clicking the Increase Indent button on the **Home** Tab. This increases the indent for this list item and the numbering or bullet character changes, too. Continue to add other second level list items, and when someone want to go back to the first level click the Decrease Indent button.

If the bullets or numbering sequences are not exactly what someone want, someone can format them to suit the needs by choosing **Home** tab > Click **Bullets/ Numbering/ Multilevel Lists button** > Select **desired bullet/ Number/ Letter/ Multilevel list type**.

The outline style that someone is currently using will be highlighted, and someone can change it by selecting another outline style and clicking OK to apply it.

With multi-level lists like this bulleted list someone can create custom bullets for each individual level.

Alternatively, someone can customize the style by clicking the Customize button. On the left someone'll see Levels: 1, 2, 3, 4 and so on. Click Level 1, and someone will see the format currently applied to the first level list item. When someone click Level 2, someone will see the style currently applied to Level 2.

Someone can change the style by selecting a different option from the Bullet Style dropdown list. For example,

☐ someone can choose a bullet style from the list or

☐ select **Define New Bullet**

☐ select a **bullet character** from the currently selected **symbol** font or from any another font

☐ click **OK**.

☐ For changing the number style, Click on the **Numbering button**

☐ Select the different number style from the **library** or click on **Define New**

Number Format

☐ Select the required format from the **drop-down** list under the heading **Number**

Style

☐ Someone can change the font type. Color and all font formatting options for the new defined number format by clicking on the Font button in the **Define New**

Number Format window

Typically, most lists only require one or two levels but, if someone need more, someone can continue and configure different bullets or numbering options for lower levels. When someone is done click OK and the list will be formatted using the new design.

Multiple Lines

When someone need a new line, but someone don't want that line to have a bullet or a number, hold the Shift key down when someone press Enter. This adds a new line but without a bullet or number, and someone can continue to do this to type multiple lines with just one bullet or number. For example, if the bullet item is "Handbooks" and someone want to list the various types — IT, HR and Admin — under the Handbook bullet. When someone is ready for the next number or bullet, press Enter without the Shift key.

Create Step-By-Step Lists

For step-by-step lists someone can configure the numbering so that the word Step automatically replaces each number.

☐ First, create a numbered list.

☐ Next select the list text, and

☐ Click Multilevel List button

☐ Click on **Define new multilevel list/ Define New list Style** option. Make the changes in the list levels as per the requirement/ Create a new label for the list.

☐ Click **OK**.

Or

or

Moving List Item

One advantage to numbered lists is that someone can reorder the item in the list and the numbering changes accordingly. So, if someone move a paragraph up or down the list, the numbers will change depending on the paragraph's position in the list. To move a

paragraph use **Alt + Shift** and the **Up or Down** arrow keys.

Whenever someone need to type a series of item marked with numbers or bullets, someone will find Word's bulleted and numbered list options a useful tool for formatting the data.

3.4 BORDERS AND SHADING

Borders are rules someone can add to any or all of the four sides of a paragraph. Shading is the color or artistic design someone use as background for a paragraph. Borders and shading are formatting tools for enhancing text, paragraphs, table cells or frames. Commonly used borders and shading effects can be quickly added to text, paragraphs, frames and tables or table elements, using the Tables and Borders toolbar, or someone can choose from a comprehensive list of borders and shading styles using the Borders and

Shading dialog box. Borders or shading applied to a paragraph will usually affect the entire paragraph, extending from the left indent to the right indent, even if the paragraph contains no or a very short line of text. If someone are not comfortable with the horizontal span of the effects of the borders or shading applied, someone should adjust the indent markers on the ruler.

To change the entire page color with desired color.

☐ Go to **Page Lay out** tab

☐ Click on the **Page Color** Button

☐ Select color someone want to apply to entire page

Apply Border to entire page/s

☐ On the **Page Lay out** tab, click **Page Borders** button. The Borders and Shading dialog box will be displayed.

☐ Click the **Page Borders** tab to display the Page Borders options page.
o Under Setting, click any of Box, **Shadow**, or **3-D**, if someone want border line on all four sides of the selected item.

- In the **Style** list, click a desired line for the border style someone want.

- In the **Color** box, click the line color someone want for the border.

- In the **Width** box, click the line width someone want for the border.

- To change individual border lines to a new style, color, or width, first click **Custom**, then click the Style, Color, and Width settings someone want, and then click the border buttons in the **Preview** diagram to apply the new options.

☐ In the **Apply to** box, click the item on which to apply the borders and shading formatting settings someone have selected.

☐ Click OK.

Adding Borders Using Borders and Shading Dialog Box

The Borders and Shading dialog box enables someone to select from a list of preset or custom borders and shading styles to add to selected text, paragraphs, etc.

☐ Select the paragraph(s), cells, graphics, etc, to which someone want to add borders.

☐ On the **Page Layout** tab, click **Page Borders** button. The Borders and Shading dialog box will be displayed.

☐ Click the **Borders** tab to display the **Borders** options page.

o Under Setting, click any of Box, **Shadow**, or **3-D**, if someone want border line on all four sides of the selected item.

- In the **Style** list, click a desired line for the border style someone want.
- In the **Color** box, click the line color someone want for the border.
- In the **Width** box, click the line width someone want for the border.
- To change individual border lines to a new style, color, or width, first

click **Custom**, then click the Style, Color, and Width settings someone want, and then click the border buttons in the **Preview** diagram to apply the new options.

☐ In the **Apply to** box, click the item on which to apply the borders and shading

formatting settings someone have selected.

☐ Click OK.

Removing Borders

Just as easily as someone added borders to item in a document, someone can also remove the borders any time such borders no longer appeal to someone. Someone can easily change such borders in the same approach. Follow the steps enumerated below to remove borders from item:

☐ Select the paragraph(s), table cells, frames, or graphics someone want to remove borders from.

☐ On the **Home** tab, click the arrow next to the **Border** button and click **No Border**

.

☐ Alternatively, on the **Page Lay out** tab, click **Page Borders**.

☐ From the **Borders and Shading** dialog box, click the **Borders** tab, under

☐ **Setting**, click **None** and then click **OK**.

Adding Shading Using the Borders and Shading Dialog Box

☐ Select the paragraphs, cells, graphics, or frames to which someone want to add shading.

☐ On the **Page Layout** tab, click **Page Borders**.

☐ From the **Borders and Shading** dialog box, Click the **Shading** tab.

☐ Do one or more of the following:

• from the color palette under Fill, click the fill color someone want for the shading. If someone want additional colors, click the More Colors button.

• In the Style box, click a shading style to be applied over the fill color. (Click Clear to apply only the Fill color, click Solid to apply only the

pattern color, or click any pattern style to apply both fill and pattern

colors.)

• In the **Color** box, click a color for the lines and dots in the shading

pattern someone selected. This box will not be available if Clear is the current selection in the Style box.

☐ In the **Apply to** box, click the appropriate item on which to apply the shading formatting.

☐ Click the OK button

Removing Shading/Shading Settings

1. Select the text, paragraphs, cells, graphics, or frames from which someone want to remove shading.

2. On the **Page Lay out** tab, click **Page Borders**.

3. From the **Borders and Shading** dialog box, Click the **Shading** tab.

4. Do one or both of the following:

☐ To rid the current selection of any fill color applied, click **No Fill**,

under **Fill**.

☐ To rid the current selection of any styles applied, click **Clear** in

the Style box, under Patterns.

2. In the **Apply to** box, select an appropriate option.

3. Click **OK**.

Change the Width of a Bordered or Shaded Area in a Paragraph

Borders and shading applied to a paragraph are added relative to the indents, so that the shading and border lines extend from the left indent of the selected paragraph to the right indent of the paragraph. Even if the selected paragraph contains only a short line of text, or no text at all, borders and shading added will always extend from the left indent of the selected paragraph to the right indent of the paragraph. Using the indent markers on the horizontal ruler, someone can easily adjust the width of the bordered or shaded area in a paragraph containing short lines of text, to enhance its beauty. Here are the steps someone should follow to change the width of the bordered or shaded area in a paragraph with short lines of text.

3.5 Adjusting the width of a bordered or shaded area in a paragraph with a short line of text

1. Position the insertion points in the paragraph with short lines of text to display the indent markers for that paragraph on the ruler.

2. Drag the indent markers on the horizontal ruler to adjust the width of the bordered or shaded area.

For a left-aligned paragraph, I'll recommend someone drag the right-indent marker to adjust the width of the bordered or shaded area in the paragraph; and for a right-aligned paragraph, drag the small box below the left-indent marker; while for a centered paragraph, I'll recommend someone adjust the width appropriately from left and right, by dragging the small box below the left indent marker to move the left and first-line indent markers, and then drag the right-indent marker proportionately.

Paragraphs with different alignments showing adjusted borders above a paragraph with a short line of text

Tips:

☐ To change an individual border line to a different or new style, weight, or color, first click the Line Style, Line Weight, and Border Color settings someone want, and then click the border buttons representing the borderline someone want the settings applied to. In other words, to add or change settings for the entire border or individual border line, follow step (i) through (iv) above in order.

☐ The only type of border formatting someone can apply to ordinary text (portion of text in a paragraph, other than the entire paragraph) is Outside Border. No matter the type of available border someone click, except No Border, Word applies the Outside Border formatting to the partial text of the paragraph someone selected.

☐ The only types of border someone can apply to a selected paragraph are: Outside Border, Left Border, Top Border, Right Border, and Bottom Border.

☐ To apply the Horizontal Line border formatting, make sure no text is selected. If someone select an item before clicking the Horizontal Line border type, the selected item will be overtyped (overwritten).

3.6 SUMMARY

In this chapter, we have discussed about managing files and word documents. Also we have discussed about setting lists and shading and borders to the selected paragraphs as well as entire document.

Adding flair to the documents is great, but no one will give someone their business or publish the paper because of the color of the text or the effects on the pie chart. Effective document design is about helping the important information stand out. Someone can also mix and match theme colors, fonts, and effects to quickly create the own look. Select separate theme color, theme font, and theme effect sets from them respective galleries on the Page Layout tab.

Cover pages are always inserted at the beginning of a document, regardless of where the cursor appears in the document. Someone can quickly and easily give the document a professional look by applying a document theme. A document theme is a set of formatting choices that include a set of theme colors, a set of theme fonts (including heading and body text fonts), and a set of theme effects (including lines and fill effects).

Getting started with a basic document in Microsoft Office Word 2016 is as easy as opening a new blank document and starting to type. Word's **Save As**... feature is a great way to save multiple versions of the same file. Someone can easily preserve earlier versions of the document if someone think someone will need to go back to an earlier stage. One drawback of saving multiple versions of the same file under different names is it can become difficult to manage all the files and it can use a considerable amount of storage space.

A list is a good way to organize item in a document because it forces someone to work in a compressed and shortened format, which makes the writing easier to read. Someone can use lists for everything from step-by-step instructions to a series of points that someone want to make and more. When writing step-by-step instructions, be sure to use a verb as the first word in the instructions. This forces someone to be even more succinct. Borders are rules someone can add to any or all of the four sides of a paragraph. Shading is the color or artistic design someone use as background for a paragraph. Borders and shading are formatting tools for enhancing text, paragraphs, table cells or frames.

Commonly used borders and shading effects can be quickly added to text, paragraphs, frames and tables or table elements, using the Tables and Borders toolbar, or someone can choose from a comprehensive list of borders and shading styles using the Borders and Shading dialog box. Borders or shading applied to a paragraph will usually affect the entire paragraph, extending from the left indent to the right indent, even if the paragraph contains no or a very short line of text. If someone are not comfortable with the horizontal span of the effects of the borders or shading applied, someone should adjust the indent markers on the ruler.

Chapter 4

Paragraph Formatting

4.1 INTRODUCTION

Wouldn't it be nice to know that the documents will always look the way someone intended, whether on screen, printed, or e-mailed? Well, one of the best ways to guarantee the appearance of the documents is also one of the easiest: strong, solid, simple paragraph formatting.

As someone know, Word is all about keeping things simple. No matter how complex the document's content, the least complicated solution to any task will always give someone more precise, impressive results than convoluted workarounds that take three times the effort! A quick overview of paragraph formatting provides one of the best examples of this core Word concept.

3 levels of formatting

Someone might know that Word organizes most document formatting into three levels (font, paragraph, and section). Paragraph formatting, the second of these and the basic building block of most documents, includes tasks such as paragraph spacing, line spacing, alignment, paragraph borders and shading, bullets and numbering, and indents and tabs.

When someone apply paragraph formatting to the text of the document, Word stores it in the paragraph mark (¶) that falls at the end of each paragraph. Why is this important for someone to know? Well, if the formatting of the text has ever changed when someone moved it from one part of the document to another (or between documents), formatting stored in a paragraph mark was the reason.

Formatting can change if someone move text into a paragraph that contains different formatting. Notice, in fact, the formatting smart tags that appear whenever someone paste text from one location to another in Word. These smart tags offer someone the option to keep source formatting or match destination formatting, which refers to the formatting contained in the paragraph marks at the copy source and the paste destination. Want to be even smarter than the smart tags? Easy! To steer clear of the complications of source and destination formatting, avoid leaving empty paragraphs in the document (that is, paragraph marks where there is no text). The best way to do that is to use spacing Before or After the paragraph (find this under Spacing on the Indents and Spacing tab of the Paragraph dialog box, accessible from the Format menu, Paragraph command) to automatically make space between paragraphs when someone press ENTER. Increase the paragraph spacing instead of pressing ENTER multiple times for a new paragraph and someone won't get any of this: Those ugly, empty paragraph marks aren't empty at all — they contain lots of formatting that can get in the way.

For a strong document foundation, check out more helpful tips on paragraph alignment and spacing options in the table that follows.

Paragraph alignment and spacing options Create space between paragraphs

Use paragraph spacing before or after a paragraph to create space between separate paragraphs. Just go to the Indents and Spacing tab of the Paragraph dialog box (Format menu, Paragraph command) and type the desired number of points (or use the spin boxes to make a selection) in the text boxes labeled Before or After. As a good rule of thumb, use 12 points before or after the paragraph when working with standard body text (type that has 12 pt in either the Before or After text box), to create a single line of space between the paragraphs. IMPORTANT Be sure to include the pt when someone type points before or after. Otherwise, Word might convert the entry to a line setting that is not what someone intended. Keep the document simple to edit by keeping the formatting choices as consistent as possible throughout the document. If someone choose to use space before on some paragraphs, try to stick with space before throughout. It will end up being less work than switching back and forth.

Someone might be thinking, "Why should I take the extra step to set paragraph spacing when I can just press ENTER twice to get a new paragraph?" Well, think about this: Once someone set paragraph spacing, it stays set until someone change it. So, it's a lot less work than manually making space between the paragraphs with empty paragraph marks. Paragraph spacing also gives someone more control than extra paragraph marks because someone can set the space precisely. If someone want half or a quarter of a line between paragraphs, or multiple lines, just set whatever someone need. Even adjust paragraph spacing to suit the font size by changing the number of points before or after the paragraph.

Use equal amounts of space before and after the paragraph for text in table cells, to easily center the text vertically within the cell and create the desired cell height at the same time without having to set row height or cell alignment. (For help formatting tables, see the tip sheet "Someone Don't Have to be an Architect! The Pure and Simple Logic of Building Extraordinary Tables," in Microsoft Office Document Designer.)

Create space between lines of the same paragraph
Use the line spacing feature to create space between lines of the same paragraph. Access line spacing on the Indents and Spacing tab of the Paragraph dialog box (Format menu, Paragraph command). By default, line spacing is set to Single. To change line spacing, select a different option from the drop-down list labeled Line spacing.
1.5 lines and Double line spacing are the obvious options. When someone select line spacing At least orExactly, the text box beside the Line spacing drop-down list reads 12 pt. Use the spin boxes to change the point setting, or just type in the desired number of points.At least 12 pt means that lines of the active paragraph(s) will be no less than 12 points high, regardless of text size, so text in 8 point font will have 12 point line spacing, but lines of text in 24 point font will grow to accommodate the font size. Line spacing Exactly, on the other hand, will keep the line spacing to exactly the selected number of points, regardless of font size.

If the top or bottom of text is cut off in paragraphs with a large font, line spacing set to Exactly is a likely cause!

NOTE Notice that there's a difference between single line spacing on 12 point text and line spacing of exactly 12 points. Single line spacing adds buffer space

between lines. On the other hand, when someone set exactly 12 point line spacing on 12 point text, the bottom of the text in the first line of the paragraph will almost touch the top of text in the second line, etc. When someone need to fit just a little more text on one

page, try decreasing the line spacing by setting Exactly to just a point or two larger than

the font size. The line spacing will be less than single, so someone'll get more

room, but not so much less that anyone will notice!

Align paragraphs horizontally on the page

Select paragraph alignment options to align complete paragraphs along the left

or right margins or centered between the two. Or, select justified alignment for text

that is equally distributed between the margins so that each line of the paragraph

(other than the last) is identical in length. To set paragraph alignment, either click in

the desired paragraph or select several paragraphs to format them at once. Then,

click the icon on the Formatting toolbar that corresponds to the alignment someone

want, as shown here: Someone doesn't have to push text over with indents, tabs, or the ruler

bar to change the alignment of a paragraph. A single click changes the alignment for the whole

paragraph at once (or several selected paragraphs).

NOTE If the tabs or indents seem off when someone change paragraph alignment, that's because tabs and indents are designed to work with left **Office**

Or select alignment on the Indents and Spacing tab of the Paragraph dialog box (Format menu, Paragraph command). aligned paragraphs. For more information on setting indents and tabs,

check out the tip sheet

"Do The Paragraphs Measure Up?" (Microsoft Office Document Designer).

Start a new line within the same paragraph

Use a line break (also called a soft return) to force text to start on a new line of the same

paragraph. Just place the insertion point where someone want the line to break and press

SHIFT+ENTER. When viewing formatting marks, a line break character will look like this:

Please don't use the spacebar or tabs to push text to a new line of the same paragraph! It's too much work and never works smoothly. The line break places one nonprinting character at the end of the line and that's all. One step, perfect every time. When lines of text logically go together, simplify paragraph formatting by placing line breaks instead

of paragraph returns.

The address information in a business letter, for example, is a collection of single-spaced lines that fall above the salutation,

like so:

Since there is space before and after that group of lines, use line breaks to separate them instead of paragraph marks, and just press ENTER for one paragraph mark at the end

of the group. That way, using the example here, someone have one set of

formatting in one paragraph mark instead of four sets of formatting for the same result.

4.2 TEXT PRESENTATION

The term 'Text presentation' means the way in which the text in the document gets

presented. Here Presentation means the formatting applied to the text i.e. Headings,

Paragraph spacing, line spacing etc.

In the following section we are going to discuss about How to apply, modify heading

styles to the selected text in the word document. These are inbuilt styles, but someone can modify the existing styles and also make the own heading styles. Also, we are going

to discuss about the paragraph, line spacing, indentation and page breaks, and text

alignment.

4.2.1 Add a Heading

The best way to add headings in Word is to apply styles. Someone can use the built-in

styles, or someone can customize them.

Apply a heading style

☐ Type the text of the heading, and then select it.

☐ On the **Home** tab, in the **Styles** group, click the heading style that someone want.

☐ If someone don't see the style that someone want, click the **More** button to expand the **Quick Styles gallery.**

Note: Someone can see how selected text will look with a particular style by placing the pointer over the style that someone want to preview.

Note: If the style that someone want does not appear in the Quick Styles gallery, press CTRL+SHIFT+S to open the Apply Styles task pane. Under Style Name, type the name of the style that someone want. The list shows only those styles that someone already used

in the document, but someone can type the name of any style that is defined for the document.

Customize a heading style

Someone can change the font and formatting of a heading style.

☐ Select the heading text that someone want to customize.

☐ On the Home tab, in the Styles group, click the heading style that someone want to customize.

☐ Select **Modify** option.

☐ Make the changes that someone want.

For example, someone can change the font, the size, or the color.

☐ On the **Home** tab, in the **Styles** group, right-click the heading style that someone customized, and then click **Update Heading to Match Selection**.

Every time someone apply that heading style in the document, the heading style will include the customizations.

4.2.2 Line Spacing

In Microsoft Word 2010, the default spacing for most Quick Style sets is 1.15 between lines and a blank line between paragraphs. The default spacing in Office Word 2003 documents are 1.0 between lines and no blank line between paragraphs. The 2016 default is 2.0

Change the line spacing

The easiest way to change the line spacing for an entire document is to apply a Quick

Style set that uses the spacing that someone want. If someone want to change the line

spacing for a portion of the document, someone can select the paragraphs and change their

line spacing settings.

Use a style set to change line spacing for an entire document:

☐ On the **Home** tab, in the **Styles** group, click **Change Styles**.

☐ Point to **Style Set** and point to the various style sets. Using the live preview,

notice how the line spacing changes from one style set to the next.

When someone see spacing that someone like, click the name of the style set.

Change the line spacing in a portion of the document

☐ Select the paragraphs for which someone want to change the line spacing.

☐ On the **Home** tab, in the **Paragraph** group, click **Line Spacing**.

Someone can use any of the following given methods for changing the line spacing of the

selected paragraph.

1. Select paragraph

2. Click on the **Line and Paragraph Spacing** button from **Home** tab.

3. Select the desired line spacing from the list given.

OR

☐ Select paragraph

☐ Click on the **Line and Paragraph Spacing** button from the **Home** Tab

☐ From the drop-down list, click on the **Line Spacing Options** button

From the Paragraph window that will appear on the screen, select desired line spacing

option from the drop-down list below the **Line Spacing** option or someone can customize

the spacing between lines by changing the number below the **At option.**

Note: Remember that the depending on the option selected from the **Line Spacing** list

the type of the numbers in the **At** box get changed.

For Ex.

If someone have selected the any of the Single, Multiple, or Double option the type of the number will be **the number of lines.** But if someone select the **At least** or **Exactly option,** the values will be Point size of the text. This means the line spacing will be same as the point size in the box.

4.2.3 Paragraph Spacing

Change the spacing before or after paragraphs

The easiest way to change the spacing between paragraphs for an entire document is to apply a Quick Style set that uses the spacing that someone want. If someone want to change

the spacing between paragraphs for a portion of the document, someone can select the paragraphs and change their spacing-before and spacing-after settings.

Use a style set to change paragraph spacing for an entire document

☐ On the **Home** tab, in the **Styles** group, click **Change** Styles.

☐ Point to **Style Set** and point to the various style sets.

☐ Using the live preview, notice how the line spacing changes from one style set to the next.

☐ When someone see spacing that someone like, click the name of the style set.

Change the spacing before and after selected paragraphs

By default, paragraphs are followed by a blank line, and headings have extra space above them.

☐ Select the paragraph before/ after which someone want to change the spacing.

☐ On the **Page Layout** tab, in the **Paragraph** group, under **Spacing**, click the arrow next to **Before/ After** and enter the amount of space that someone want.

4.2.4 Indentation

Indentation determines the distance of the paragraph from either the left or the right margin. Within the margins, someone can increase or decrease the indentation of a paragraph or group of paragraphs. Someone can also create a negative indent (also known as an outdent), which pulls the paragraph out toward the left margin. Someone can also create a hanging indent, in which the first line of the paragraph is not indented, but subsequent lines are.

Indent only the first line of a paragraph

☐ Click in front of the line that someone want to indent.

☐ On the Page **Lay out** tab, click the **Paragraph Dialog Box Launcher**, and then click the **Indents and Spacing** tab. OR on the **Home** tab, click on the **Line and Paragraph Spacing** button, click on the line spacing option.

☐ The paragraph window will appear on the screen.

OR

☐ In the Special list under **Indentation**, click **First line**, and then in the **By** box, set the amount of space that someone want the first line to be indented.

NOTE: The first line of the paragraph and all subsequent paragraphs that someone type will be indented. However, any paragraphs before the selected paragraph must be manually indented by using the same procedure.

Increase or decrease the left indent of an entire paragraph

☐ Select the paragraph that someone want to change.

☐ On the Page **Lay out** tab, in the **Paragraph** group, click the arrows next to Indent Left to increase or decrease the left indentation of the paragraph.

OR

☐ Use the same steps for the '**Indent only the first line of a paragraph**'

☐ In the Paragraph window, select the Indent and Spacing tab and

☐ Change the values in the boxes in front of the **Left** and **Right** options under the **Indentation** section, according to the choice.

Indent all but the first line of a paragraph

☐ Select the paragraph in which someone want to indent all but the first line of the paragraph, also referred to as a hanging indent

☐ On the horizontal ruler, drag the Hanging Indent marker to the position at which someone want the indent to start.

☐ If someone don't see the horizontal ruler that runs along the top of the document, click the **View Ruler** button at the top of the vertical scroll bar.

Use precise measurements to set a hanging indent

☐ For more precision in setting a hanging indent, someone can select options on the Indents and Spacing tab.

☐ On the Page **Layout** tab, click the **Paragraph Dialog Box** Launcher, and then click the **Indents and Spacing** tab.

☐ In the Special list under **Indentation**, click **Hanging**, and then in the **By** box, set the amount of space that someone want for the hanging indent.

Create a negative indent

☐ Select the text or paragraph that someone want to extend into the left margin.

☐ On the **Page Layout** tab, in the Paragraph group, click the **down arrow** in the **Indent Left** box.

☐ Continue to click the down arrow until the selected text is positioned where someone wants it in the left margin.

4.2.5 Alignment

Horizontal alignment determines the appearance and orientation of the edges of the paragraph: left-aligned text, right-aligned text, centered text, or justified text, which is aligned evenly along the left and right margins. For example, in a paragraph that is left aligned (the most common alignment), the left edge of the paragraph is flush with the left margin.

Align the text left or right

☐ Select the text that someone want to align.

☐ On the Home tab, in the Paragraph group, click Align Left or Align Right

Center the text

☐ Select the text that someone want to center.

☐ On the Home tab, in the Paragraph group, click Center.

Justify the text

Someone can justify the text, which might make the last line of text in a paragraph considerably shorter than the other lines.

☐ Select the text someone want to justify.

☐ On the Home tab, in the Paragraph group, click Justify.

4.3 TABS

A tab stop on a typewriter is a location where the carriage movement is halted by mechanical gears. Tab stops are set manually, and pressing the tab key causes the carriage to go to the next tab stop. In text editors on a computer, the same concept is implemented simplistically with automatic, fixed tab stops.

Modern word processors generalize this concept by offering tab stops that have an alignment attribute and cause the text to be automatically aligned at left, at right or center of the tab stop itself. Such tab stops are paragraph-specific properties and can be moved to a different location in any moment, or even removed.

Types of tab stops

- A Left Tab stop sets the start position of text that will then run to the right as someone type.

- A Center Tab stop sets the position of the middle of the text. The text centers on this position as someone type.

- A Right Tab stop sets the right end of the text. As someone type, the text moves to the left.

- A Decimal Tab stop aligns numbers around a decimal point. Independent of the number of digits, the decimal point will be in the same position. (Someone can align numbers around a decimal character only; someone cannot use the decimal tab to align numbers around a different character, such as a hyphen or an ampersand symbol.)

- A Bar Tab stop doesn't position text. It inserts a vertical bar at the tab position.

Set tab stops by using the ruler

☐ Click the tab selector at the left end of the ruler until it displays the type of tab

that someone want.

NOTE: If someone don't see the horizontal ruler that runs along the top of the document,

click the View Ruler button at the top of the vertical scroll bar.

☐ Click the ruler where someone want to set the tab stop.

Notes about using the horizontal ruler to set tab stops

☐ By default, there are no tab stops on the ruler when someone open a new blank

document.

☐ The final two options on the tab selector are actually for indents. Someone can click

these and then click the ruler to position the indents, rather than sliding the

indent markers along the ruler. Click First Line Indent , and then click the

upper half of the horizontal ruler where someone want the first line of a paragraph to

begin. Click Hanging Indent , and then click the lower half of the horizontal

ruler where someone want the second and all following lines of a paragraph to

begin.

☐ When someone set a bar tab stop, a vertical bar line appears where someone set the tab

stop (someone don't need to press the TAB key). A bar tab is similar to

strikethrough formatting, but it runs vertically through the paragraph at the

location of the bar tab stop. Like other types of tabs, someone can set a bar tab stop

before or after someone type the text of the paragraph.

☐ Someone can remove a tab stop by dragging it (up or down) off the ruler. When someone

release the mouse button, the tab stop disappears.

☐ Someone can also drag existing tab stops left or right along the ruler to a different

position.

☐ When multiple paragraphs are selected, only the tabs from the first paragraph

show on the ruler.

Set tab stops by using the Tabs dialog box

If someone want the tab stops at precise positions that someone can't get by clicking the ruler, or

if someone want to insert a specific character (leader) before the tab, someone can use the Tabs dialog box.

☐ Click the **Page Lay out** tab, click the **Paragraph Dialog Box** Launcher, and then click **Tabs**.

☐ Under **Tab** stop position, type the location where someone want to set the tab stop.

☐ Under **Alignment**, click the type of tab stop that someone want.

☐ To add dots with the tab stop, or to add another type of leader, click the option that someone want under Leader.

☐ Click Set.

☐ Repeat steps 2-5 to add another tab stop or click OK.

Add leaders, or dotted lines, between tab stops

Someone can add dot leaders between tab stops or choose other formatting options in the Tabs dialog box.

☐ Type the text that someone want to appear before the leader.

☐ On the horizontal ruler, set the tab stop that someone want.

☐ Click the **Page Layout** tab, click the **Paragraph Dialog Box** Launcher, and then click **Tabs**.

☐ Under **Leader**, click the leader option that someone want.

☐ Click **OK**, and then press TAB.

☐ When someone press ENTER to start a new line, the formatted tab stop is available on the new line.

TIP If someone want to use tab stops and dot leaders to format a table of contents, consider using Word to create a table of contents automatically.

Change the spacing between the default tab stops

If someone set manual tab stops, the default tab stops are interrupted by the manual tab stops that someone set. Manual tab stops that are set on the ruler override the default tab stop settings.

☐ Click the **Page Layout** tab, click the **Paragraph Dialog Box** Launcher

☐ In the **Paragraph** dialog box, click **Tabs**.

☐ In the **Default tab stops** box, enter the amount of spacing that someone want between the default tab stops.

☐ When someone press the TAB key, the tab will stop across the page at the distance that someone specified.

Clear tab stop spacing

If someone added manual tab stops, someone can clear the spacing for one-tab stop or for all manual tab stops. After someone clear the spacing, the tab stop characters move to default locations.

☐ On the Page Layout tab, click the Paragraph Dialog Box Launcher.

☐ In the **Paragraph** dialog box, click **Tabs**.

☐ In the list under Tab stop position, click the tab stop position that someone want to clear, and then click Clear.

TIP: To remove the spacing from all manual tab stops, click Clear All.

☐ Repeat step 3 for each tab stop position that someone want to clear.

☐ Click OK.

IMPORTANT *The tab stop characters are not removed. To remove them, someone need to delete them manually or run find and replace, with ^t in the Find what box and an empty Replace with box. To open the Find and Replace dialog box, on Home tab, in the Editing group, click Replace.*

4.4 PAGE BREAKS

Someone can insert a page break anywhere in the document, or someone can specify where Microsoft Word positions automatic page breaks.

If someone insert manual page breaks in documents that are more than several pages in length, someone might have to frequently re-break pages as someone edit the document. To avoid the difficulty of manually rebreaking pages, someone can set options to control where Word positions automatic page breaks.

Insert a manual page break

☐ Click where someone want to start a new page.

☐ On the Insert tab, in the Pages group, click Page Break.

Prevent page breaks in the middle of a paragraph

☐ Select the paragraph that someone want to prevent from breaking onto two pages.

On the **Page Layout** tab, click the **Paragraph Dialog Box** Launcher, and then click the **Line and Page Breaks** tab.

Select the **Keep lines together** check box under the **Pagination** section.

Prevent page breaks between paragraphs

Select the paragraphs that someone want to keep together on a single page.

On the **Page Layout** tab, click the **Paragraph Dialog** Box Launcher, and then click the **Line and Page Breaks** tab.

Select the **Keep with next** check box under the **Pagination** section.

Specify a page break before a paragraph

Click the paragraph that someone want to follow the page break.

On the **Page Layout** tab, click the **Paragraph Dialog** Box Launcher, and then click the **Line and Page Breaks** tab.

Select the **Page break before** check box under the **Pagination** section.

Place at least two lines of a paragraph at the top or bottom of a page

☐ On the **Page Layout** tab, click the **Paragraph Dialog** Box Launcher, and then click the **Line and Page Breaks** tab.

☐ Select the **Widow/Orphan control** check box under the **Pagination** section.

NOTE: *This option is turned on by default.*

4.5 WORKING WITH COLUMNS

Give the business newsletters, manuals and brochures a designer looks by arranging the text in them in a columnar Lay out. The shorter lines and punchier look of a two column Lay out maximizes the use of space on the page and aids readability.

Benefits of Using Columns

☐ When someone lay out page text in columns someone will generally fit a little more text on the page than if someone laid it out so the lines stretch full width of the page.

☐ The shorter lines of text are also easier to read, as the reader's eye doesn't need to travel so far across the page before returning to read the next line of text.

☐ A document laid out in columns can look more approachable too, as there is white space within the page, which offers readers a place to rest their eyes.

Setting Entire columns format for entire document

Open the word file for which someone want to set columns.

☐ Select entire text using command **Ctrl+A** or Click on **Select** button from **Home** tab and click **Select All** option

☐ Click on **Page Layout** tab

☐ Under the **Page Setup** group, click on the **Columns** Button

☐ Click on the desired columns style.

If someone wants to apply columns to the new document which does not have any text all someone need to do is open the new document and follow steps 2 to 4.

If someone wants to apply the columns to only selected paragraph/s, then select the desired paragraph/s and follow steps 2 to 4.

Someone can apply column separator line then:

☐ Select the text someone want to set columns for or select entire document as per the desire.

☐ Click on **Page Layout** tab

☐ Under the **Page Setup** group, click on the **Columns** Button.

☐ Click on **More Columns** Option

☐ **Columns** window will appear on the screen

☐ Click in the **check box** besides the option **Line Between**

Vertical line will appear in between the columns as a separator for selected paragraph or entire document.

Someone can also set the number of columns as per the choice by changing the number in the text box besides the **Number of Columns** option. Someone can also customize the width and spacing of the columns as per the judgment/ requirement by changing the values in the boxes under the section **Width and Spacing.**

4.6 Keyboard shortcuts

Here are some keyboard shortcuts to use when formatting paragraphs.

Ctrl+E Applies center alignment.

Ctrl+J Applies justified alignment.

Ctrl+Shift+J Spreads the current paragraph across the entire width between the margins.

Ctrl+M Increases the indentation of the current paragraph or selected paragraphs to the next tab stop.

Ctrl+Shift+M Decreases the indentation to the preceding tab stop.

Ctrl+Q Resets the paragraph formatting to the default paragraph formatting of the applied style.

Ctrl+R Applies right alignment.

Ctrl+Shift+S In Word 2010 and Word 2016, opens the **Apply Styles** task pane for applying, creating, or modifying styles and formatting (use**Alt+Ctrl+Shift+S** to modify a style without applying it to the selection). In Word 2003, selects the **Styles** drop-down list on the **Formatting** toolbar, if the **Formatting** toolbar is displayed, or opens the **Style** dialog box.

Alt+Ctrl+Shift+S Opens the **Styles** pane (Word 2010 and Word 2016).

Ctrl+1 Applies single line spacing to the current paragraph or selected paragraphs.

Ctrl+2 Applies double spacing to the current paragraph or selected paragraphs.

Ctrl+5 Applies 1.5 line spacing to the current paragraph or selected paragraphs.

Ctrl+0 Adds or removes additional space before the current paragraph or selected paragraphs.

Shift+F1 In Word 2010 and Word 2016, shows or hides the formatting properties in the task pane. In Word 2003, shows the **Show Formatting** task pane.

F4 Redoes the last action performed.

4.7 SUMMARY

In this chapter we have discussed about the various features of Microsoft Word for paragraph formatting. As someone know, Word is all about keeping things simple. No matter how complex the document's content, the least complicated solution to any task will always give someone more precise, impressive results than convoluted workarounds that take three times the effort! A quick overview of paragraph formatting provides one of the best examples of this core Word concept.

The term 'Text presentation' means the way in which the text in the document gets presented. Here Presentation means the formatting applied to the text i.e. Headings, Paragraph spacing, line spacing etc.

Here we have discussed about How to apply, modify heading styles to the selected text in the word document. These are inbuilt styles, but someone can modify the existing styles and also make the own heading styles. Also have discussed about the paragraph, line spacing, indentation and page breaks, and text alignment.

A tab stop on a typewriter is a location where the carriage movement is halted by mechanical gears. Tab stops are set manually, and pressing the tab key causes the carriage to go to the next tab stop. In text editors on a computer, the same concept is implemented simplistically with automatic, fixed tab stops.

Someone can insert a page break anywhere in the document, or someone can specify where Microsoft Word positions automatic page breaks.

If someone insert manual page breaks in documents that are more than several pages in length, someone might have to frequently re-break pages as someone edit the document. To avoid the difficulty of manually re-breaking pages, someone can set options to control where Word positions automatic page breaks.

Someone can give the business newsletters, manuals and brochures a designer look by arranging the text in them in a columnar Lay out. The shorter lines and punchier look of a two-column Lay out maximizes the use of space on the page and aids readability.

Chapter 5

Tables

5.1 INTRODUCTION

Data presented in the tabular form gives better present-ability and clarity. The instructions that follow will demonstrate someone how to create a table and how to take advantage of it. The first thing, to be known is that someone can enter several rows of text in the same cell of the table. It's not necessary to count the number of rows that will go to a table but a number of "cells". For example: the advantages and the disadvantages or to compare several options.

Benefits of using tables in Microsoft Word:

☐ Tables help someone format and organize complex data and present it as part of a publication.

☐ Tables can be used as a Lay out tool, where someone can insert and format text or graphics without complicated publishing software.

5.2 INSERT A TABLE

☐ From the **Insert** tab click on the **Table** button

☐ Click on the **Insert Table** Option.

A window will appear asking someone for the number of columns and rows that someone need for the table. Enter the numbers that someone need. Someone can later add or remove rows or columns.

☐ For this example, write 5 in the box of the number of columns and rows.

☐ Press the OK button.

There is another way of inserting a table into a document; by using the button insert table.

Tables / 117

☐ Press the button.

☐ Press the left mouse button and select the numbers of columns and rows required.

☐ Release the mouse button when it's shown the size that someone want.

If someone don't see the borders of the cells of the table:

☐ Select the table

☐ go to the **Table Tools** tab

☐ click on the **Design** tab

☐ click on **Borders** drop down list

☐ select the **required border**

Someone can also change table border thickness, border style, border color, table shading color, and various inbuilt table designs by using the options given on the **Design** tab.

When the border of the table consists of dotted rows, it means that no border will be shown in the printing.

5.3 CHANGE THE WIDTH OF COLUMNS

There are two ways to change the width of a column: by using the ruler for tables or by using the menu Format. Both ways will be explained. The first will be by using the ruler.

☐ Click or place the cursor in the first cell of the table

Above the text, there is a ruler as that appears. It's used to change the width of columns and also margins inside cells. The first triangle at the top of the bar pointing downward serves for adjusting the left margin of the first row of the cell. The triangle of the left lower corner serves for adjusting the left margin besides of the text of the cell. The triangle in the lower right corner serves for adjusting the right margin of all the text of the cell.

Here is the procedure to change the width of a column by using the mouse.

☐ Place the cursor on the separator of column that is between the first and the second column on the toolbar of tables.

To recognize it, it's the checkerboard that separates each of the columns. Attention not to take inadvertently the triangle of the right margin. The cursor will change format. The cursor will be now a horizontal bar with a point in every extremity.

☐ Press and hold the left mouse button and move slowly the cursor to the right.

☐ Release the mouse button when the width of the column is about the double(copy) of what it was before.

It is to note that columns in the right-hand side of the column that someone chose fit automatically not to exceed the margins of the page. By selecting a column, someone can change its just width a little or a lot according to the needs. Someone can also give a fixed width in a column.

☐ Place the cursor in the column that someone want to change the width.

☐ In menu bar, under the **Table Tools** tab select **Lay out** tab

☐ Someone can change the width of the cell/ column by changing the value in the **Height/ Width** box.

Or

☐ Place the cursor in the cell/ column someone want and press the **right** button of the mouse **(Right Click in cell)**

☐ Click on the **Table Properties** button

☐ Click on the **Columns** tab

☐ Change the value in the **preferred** width box.

Using any of the methods discussed above someone can change the width of the column/ cell of the table in the word document.

5.4 ADD A ROW

Someone can add a row above or below selected row in a table using following steps:

☐ Place the cursor in the cell above/ below which someone want to add a row.

☐ go to the **Table Tools** tab

☐ click on the **Lay out** tab

☐ click on '**Insert Above**'/ '**Insert Below**' button.

☐ Single row will get inserted above/ below the selected row.

If someone want to add multiple rows, repeat the steps till someone add the desired number of rows.

5.5 ADD A COLUMN

Someone can add a column in the left or right side of the selected Column in a table using following steps:

☐ Place the cursor in the cell on whose left/ right someone want to add a column.

☐ go to the **Table Tools** tab

☐ click on the **Lay out** tab

☐ click on '**Insert Left'/ 'Insert Right**' button.

☐ Single column will get inserted to the left/ right side of the selected cell

If someone want to add multiple columns, repeat the steps till someone add the desired number of columns

5.6 DELETE ROW / COLUMN/ CELL/ TABLE

Follow the following steps to delete row/s, column/s or entire table:

☐ Place the cursor in the cell which row/ column someone want to delete. Or select the number of rows/ columns someone want to delete.

☐ go to the **Table Tools** tab

☐ click on the **Lay out** tab

☐ click on **Delete** button.

☐ Click on the desired option i.e. **Delete Rows, Delete Columns, or Delete Table**.

If someone want to delete only selected cells:

☐ Select the cells

☐ go to the **Table Tools** tab

☐ click on the **Lay out** tab

☐ click on **Delete** button.

☐ Click on the **Delete Cells** option.

Delete Cells Window will appear on the screen

☐ Select the desired option

☐ Click o

☐ The Selected cells get deleted and replaced with the cells to the right side or below the deleted cells

5.7 MERGE / SPLIT CELLS

Someone can merge multiple cells of the table using the following steps:

☐ Select the number of cell someone want to merge

☐ Go the **Lay out** tab on the **Table Tools** tab

☐ Click on the **Merge Cells** button

☐ All the selected cells will get combined in a single cell

If someone want to split a cell in to multiple cells use the following steps:

☐ Select the cell someone want to split

☐ Go the **Lay out** tab on the **Table Tools** tab

☐ Click on the **Split Cells** button

☐ Split Cells window will appear. Select the number of rows and columns in which someone want to split the selected cell.

☐ Click ok

☐ The selected cell will get split in the selected number of rows and columns.

If someone want to split entire table into two follow the steps given below:

☐ Select the cell after which someone the someone want to split the table

☐ Go the **Lay out** tab on the **Table Tools** tab

☐ Click on the **Split Table** button

☐ The table will get split into two tables.

5.8 DRAW A TABLE

The previous part of this page explained the "formal" way of creating a table. With this version of Word, it's possible "to draw" a table. That is to elaborate quickly a table that answers exactly the needs without going through a long series of instructions.

☐ Click on **Insert** tab

☐ Click **Table** button

☐ Select **Draw Table** option. Someone mouse cursor will get changed into a penci shape.

☐ Now someone can draw the table as per the desire with any size of rows and columns.

To begin a new table:

☐ Press the button.

☐ Place the cursor in the place where someone want to begin the new table.

☐ Press and hold the left mouse button and move the mouse to create the first

cell of the table.

This cell can then be cut in several smaller cells where the other cells can there

become attached to the left, to the right-hand side or below this one.

To cut a cell in two:

☐ Press the button.

☐ Place the cursor on the border of the cell in the place where someone want to cut

the cell in two.

☐ Press and hold the left mouse button and move the cursor towards the

opposite border of the cell.

Someone can cut a cell horizontally or vertically. Someone can even cut a cell several times.

The

cut does have to be exactly in the middle of the cell.

To erase a row or to merge two cells those are next to each other.

☐ Press the button.

☐ "Delete" the row too.

This will not just erase a border. It will merge both cells to become one. It is better

sometimes to present data on tabular form. The instructions that follow, will

demonstrate, how to create a table and take advantage of it. The first thing is that someone

can enter several rows of text in the same cell of the table. It is not necessary to count the

number of rows that will go into a table but a number of "cells". For example: the advantages

and the disadvantages or comparing several options.

5.9 SUMMARY

In this chapter we have discussed about dealing with tables in the word document. We have discussed about various aspect related to tables which are enlisted below:

☐ Insert a table

☐ Change the width of columns

☐ Add a row

☐ Add a column

☐ Delete row/ column/ Cell/ Table

☐ Merge cells

☐ Draw a table

Chapter 6

6.1 INTRODUCTION

In the past thirty years, advances in word processing software have brought unprecedented abilities to the average person. It is now possible for anyone with a computer and printer to produce high quality, professional looking documents with a minimum of effort. While today's word processing Microsoft falls short of desk top publishing software, their features are light years from those of a typewriter. Of course, to achieve the most professional looking results from the work, someone does have to know how to get the most out of the features.

The first thing that will detract from the presentation of the document and give someone away as a word processing novice is a poorly set-up page: The margins and the printed text's position on the page are the first things someone viewing the document will notice. That's why someone should pay a considerable amount of attention to these things.

Fortunately, Microsoft Word places all the page setup controls in one convenient place, the aptly titled Page Setup dialog box, so someone can make all the changes in one fell swoop. These are just some of the options someone can change in the Page Setup dialog box, but if someone master these, someone is well on the way to producing professional quality work and displaying the word processing prowess.

6.2 PAGE VIEWS

This topic, explains the different ways in which a document can be viewed in MICROSOFT Word

depending on the purpose for which it is viewed.

The different document views are explained in the section below:

Normal/ Draft View

Under **Normal** View, someone can display a single page with simple text formatting but without any drawings, comments or columns.

This view is useful for quickly entering text and for simple and basic text editing purposes.

Web Lay out View

In **Web Lay out** View, MICROSOFT Word displays page width, format and text position as it would appear on the web.

This view is useful for testing a page under a simulated web environment. This view would be especially useful when someone are using MICROSOFT Word for developing web page Layout.

Print Lay out View

Under MICROSOFT Word Document Views, **Print Lay out** View is the most frequently used Lay out.

This view is useful for ensuring that what-someone-see-on-screen is what-someone-get-in-print.

This view is also used as a proofing method before it is sent to the printer.

Outline View

In **Outline** View, MICROSOFT Word displays the headings and sub-headings providing an easy way to plan and organize the document.

This view is used for structuring the content of the document at a broad level and arranging the document in various sections and sub-sections.

Full Screen

Full Screen document view does not have a corresponding icon in the View Controls.

This option is available from Menu Toolbar. Please choose View from the Menu Toolbar and then Full Screen.

In this view, the typed matter occupies the full screen without cluttering the screen with icons, toolbars, etc. This gives someone more space for the matter.

Reading Lay out

Starting from Microsoft Office Word XP and later, the facility of reading Lay out has been provided. Under reading Lay out of the MICROSOFT Word Document Views, a document is displayed in full-page view with thumbnail images of pages for easy navigation.

This view will be helpful when someone want to read through the document as it is more reading friendly.

Document Map

"Document Map" is another view that does not have a corresponding icon in View Controls. This option is also available from Menu Toolbar. Please choose View from the Menu Toolbar and then Document Map.

Document Map displays the document in two frames. Left frame shows someone various headings in the document and the right frame shows someone the document. Someone can quickly skip to various areas of the document by clicking the headings on the right frame.

6.3 PAGE SETUP

Word offers someone several options to change the presentation of the text such as to put the text in bold, in italic or in underlined. It's also possible to change the font as well as cuts it letters and its colors from the others. The pagination allows someone to control the options of presentation of the document on paper. Someone can change the margins, the size(format) of the paper, the orientation of the paper and the other options that will be explained more low on this page.

☐ From the **File** tab, select the **Print** option

☐ From the list click on the **Page setup** option at the **bottom right corner** of the print pane.

☐ The Page Setup window will appear on the screen.

☐ Click on the **Margins** tab.

Under this tab, someone can control the margins of the document as well as the place of the heading and the foot of page inside the superior margins and subordinates. The option of **Gutter Position** is to set a supplementary space of the **Left**-hand/ **Top** side to be able to connect the document. Someone can set the Gutter by changing the value in the **Box** besides **Gutter** label.

The option **Apply To** is important too. It's from this option that someone apply the changes that someone brought to the margins or to the other options for the **Whole document** or only from the place where is the cursor at this moment. If someone use the option "**From this point** ", it forces the addition of a jump of section. This option is very important for the structure of the document. It's explained in detail on the page of the other options of Word.

☐ Click on the **Paper** tab.

From this window, someone can change the size (format) of the paper as well as its orientation. It's especially necessary to pay attention to the size (format) of the paper. Some notice too late that they have the bad size (format) of paper. Generally, the size (format) of the paper is in "A4" when it should be for the size (format) "US Letter ". The size (format) A4 is the one that is used in Europe and not in North America. Make sure to have the right size (format) before continuing or even beginning a new document. Otherwise, someone'll not only have to change the size (format) of the paper but also the presentation of the document.

☐ Click on the **Lay out** tab.

Under this tab, there are several options to control the arrangement of the text on the page. From these, there is a place of the debuts of section. I don't see the advantage of this option because someone may insert a jump of section any time and the necessary type from the Insert menu.

The options in the category of Headers and the feet of page are more interesting. They are used when someone print first side reverse. For example, the place of the numbering of pages can be different on an even page that on an odd page. With the option "different Front page ", the heading of the front page of the document can have supplementary elements such as the corporate logo and the address of the company. This heading will not be on the other pages of the document. Someone can put another heading for the rest of the document.

The option of vertical adaptation brings the advantage of power to center vertically the contents of the page. It's now useless to try to center manually. This is very advantageous for the page an picture, but not titles of the document or for a page with a table or for a common page. The option "Height" is generally used for the rest of the document.

To end, there is an option for the numbering of rows. It is rarely used, unless being paid among rows of text.

6.4 PAGE NUMBERING, HEADER AND FOOTER

Add page numbers and headers and footers by using the gallery, or create a custom page number, header, or footer.

For best results, decide first whether someone want only a page number or whether someone want information plus a page number in the header or footer. If someone want a page number and no other information, add a page number. If someone want a page number plus other information, or if someone just want the other information, add a header or footer.

6.4.1 Add a page number without any other information

If someone want a page number on each page, and someone don't want to include any other information, such as the document title or the location of the file, someone can quickly add a page number from the gallery, or someone can create a custom page number or a custom page number that includes the total number of pages (page X of Y pages).

Add a page number from the gallery

☐ On the **Insert** tab, in the **Header & Footer** group, click **Page Number**.

☐ Click the page number location that someone want.

☐ In the gallery, scroll through the options, and then click the page number format that someone want.

☐ To return to the body of the document, click **Close** Header and Footer on the **Design tab** (under Header & Footer Tools).

Office Automation / 140

Note: *The Page Number gallery includes page X of Y pages formats, in which Y is the total number of pages in the document.*

6.4.2 Add a custom page number

☐ **Double-click** in the **header** area or the **footer** area (near the top of the pag or near the bottom of the page).

☐ This opens the **Design** tab under **Header & Footer Tools**.

☐ To place the page number in the center or on the right side of the page, do the following:

- To place the page number in the **center**, click Insert **Alignment Tab** in the Position group of the **Design** tab, click **Center**, and then click **OK**.

- To place the page number on the **right** side of the page, click **Insert Alignment** Tab in the **Position** group of the **Design** tab, click **Right**, and then click **OK**. Samsung Galaxy S8 SM-G950FD Dual Sim (FACTORY UNLOCKED)

☐ On the Insert tab, in the **Text** group, click **Quick Parts**, and then click **Field**.

☐ In the **Field names** list, click **Page**, and then click **OK**.

☐ To change the numbering format, click **Page Number** in the **Header & Footer** group, and then click **Format Page Numbers**.

☐ To return to the body of the document, click **Close Header and Footer** on the **Design** tab (under Header & Footer Tools)

6.4.3 Add a custom page number that includes the total number of pages

The gallery includes some page numbers that include the total page numbers (page X of Y pages). However, if someone want to create a custom page number, do the following:

Follow all the steps in section above (i.e. 6.5.2 **Add a custom page number) then**

☐ After the page number, type a space, type of, and then type another space.

☐ On the Insert tab, in the Text group, click **Quick Parts**, and then click **Field**.

☐ In the **Field names** list, click **NumPages**, and then click **OK**.

☐ After the total number of pages, type a space, and then type pages.

☐ To change the numbering format, click **Page Number** in the **Header & Footer** group, and then click **Format Page Numbers**.

☐ To return to the body of the document, click **Close Header and Footer** on the **Design** tab (under Header & Footer Tools).

6.4.4 Start numbering with 1 on a different page

Someone can start numbering on the second page of the document, or someone can start numbering on a different page.

Start numbering on the second page

☐ **Double**-click the page number.

☐ This opens the **Design** tab under **Header & Footer Tools**.

☐ On the **Design** tab, in the **Options** group, select the **Different First Page** check box.

☐ To start numbering with 1, click **Page Number** in the **Header & Footer** group, then click **Format Page Numbers**, and then click **Start** at and enter 1.

☐ To return to the body of the document, click **Close Header and Footer** on the **Design** tab (under **Header & Footer Tools**).

6.4.5 Start numbering on a different page

To start numbering on a different page, instead of on the first page of the document, someone need to add a section break before the page where someone want to begin numbering.

☐ Click at the beginning of the page where someone want to begin numbering.

☐ Someone can press **HOME** to make sure that someone is at the start of the page.

☐ On the **Page Layout** tab, in the **Page Setup** group, click **Breaks**.

☐ Under Section **Breaks**, click **Next Page**.

☐ **Double**-click in the **header** area or the **footer** area (near the top of the page or near the bottom of the page).

☐ This opens the **Header & Footer Tools** tab.

☐ On the **Header & Footer Tools**, in the **Navigation** group, click **Link to Previous** to turn it off.

Follow the instructions for adding a page number or for adding a header and footer with a page number.

☐ To start numbering with 1, click Page Number in the Header & Footer group, then click Format Page Numbers, and then click Start at and enter 1.

☐ To return to the body of the document, click Close Header and Footer on the Design tab (under Header & Footer Tools).

6.4.6 Add different headers and footers or page numbers in different parts of the document

Someone can add page numbers to only part of the document. Someone can also use different numbering formats in different parts of the document.

For example, maybe someone want i, ii, iii numbering for the table of contents and introduction, and someone want 1, 2, 3 numbering for the rest of the document, and then no page numbers for the index.

Someone can also have different headers or footers on odd and even pages.

Add different headers and footers or page numbers on odd and even pages

☐ **Double**-click in the header area or the footer area (near the top of the page or near the bottom of the page).

This opens the **Header & Footer** Tools tab.

☐ On the Header & Footer Tools tab, in the **Options** group, select the **Different Odd & Even Pages** check box.

☐ On one of the odd pages, add the header, footer, or page numbering that someone want on odd pages.

☐ On one of the even pages, add the header, footer, or page number that someone want on even pages.

6.4.7 Add a header or footer that includes a page number

If someone want to add a graphic or text at the top or the bottom of the document, someone need to add a header or a footer. Someone can quickly add a header or a footer from the galleries, or someone can add a custom header or footer.

'Someone can use these same steps to add a header or footer without page numbers.'

Add a header or footer from the gallery

☐ On the **Insert** tab, in the **Header & Footer** group, click **Header** or **Footer**.

☐ Click the **header** or **footer** that someone want to add to the document.

☐ To return to the body of the document, click **Close Header and Footer** on the **Design** tab (under Header & Footer Tools) .

Add a custom header or footer

☐ Double-click in the **header** area or the **footer** area (near the top of the page or near the bottom of the page).

This opens the **Design** tab under **Header & Footer Tools**.

☐ To place information in the center or on the right side of the page, do any of the following:

o To place information in the center, click **Insert Alignment** Tab in the **Position** group of the **Design** tab, click **Center**, and then click **OK**.

o To place information on the right side of the page, click **Insert Alignment** Tab in the **Position** group of the **Design** tab, click **Right**, and then click **OK**.

Do one of the following:

☐ Type the information that someone want in the header.

☐ Add a field code by clicking the Insert tab, clicking **Quick Parts**, clicking **Field**, and then clicking the field someone want in the **Field** names list.

☐ Examples of information that someone can add by using fields include **Page** (for page number), **NumPages** (for the total number of pages in the document), and **FileName** (someone can include the file path).

☐ If someone add a **Page** field, someone can change the numbering format by clicking Page Number in the Header & Footer group, and then clicking Format Page Numbers.

☐ To return to the body of the document, click **Close Header and Footer** on the **Design** tab (under **Header & Footer** Tools).

Custom Header and footers

Someone can also add customized header and footer to the document where someone can put customized text, WordArt, even picture or clipArt.

Click on the header or footer part of the document and place the text, WordArt, picture etc. as per the desire.

FOOTER

HEADER

6.4.8 Remove page numbers, headers, and footers

☐ **Double**-click the header, footer, or page number.

☐ Select the header, footer, or page number.

☐ Press **DELETE** button on the keyboard

☐ Repeat **steps 1-3** in each section that has a different header, footer, or page number.

6.5 FOOTNOTES AND ENDNOTES

Footnotes and endnotes are used in printed documents to explain, comment on, or provide references for text in a document. Someone might use footnotes for detailed comments and endnotes for citation of sources.

A footnote or an endnote consists of two linked parts — the note reference mark and the corresponding note text.

NOTE: If someone want to create a bibliography, someone can find commands for creating and managing sources and citations on the References tab in the Citations & Bibliography group.

6.5.1 Insert a footnote or an endnote

Microsoft Word automatically numbers footnotes and endnotes for someone. Someone can use a single numbering scheme throughout a document, or someone can use different numbering schemes within each section in a document.

Commands for inserting and editing footnotes and endnotes can be found on the References tab in the Footnotes group.

When someone add, delete, or move notes that are automatically numbered, Word renumbers the footnote and endnote reference marks.

NOTE If the footnotes in the document are numbered incorrectly, the document may contain tracked changes. Accept the tracked changes so that Word will correctly number the footnotes and endnotes.

☐ In **Print Lay out** view click where someone want to insert the note reference mark.

☐ On the **References** tab, in the **Footnotes** group, click **Insert Footnote** or **Insert Endnote**. Word inserts the note reference mark and places the insertion point in the text area of the new footnote or endnote.

Keyboard shortcut: To insert a footnote, press **CTRL+ALT+F**. To insert an endnote, press **CTRL+ALT+D**.

By default, Word places footnotes at the end of each page and endnotes at the end of the document.

☐ Type the note text.

☐ **Double**-click the footnote or endnote reference mark to return to the reference mark in the document.

☐ To change the location or format of footnotes or endnotes, click the **Footnote & Endnote Dialog Box Launcher**, and do one of the following:

- To convert footnotes to endnotes or endnotes to footnotes, under **Location** choose either **Footnotes or Endnotes** and then click **Convert**. In the **Convert Notes** dialog box, click **OK**.

- To change the numbering format, click the desired formatting in the **Number format** box and click **Apply**.

- To use a custom mark instead of a traditional number format, click **Symbol** next to **Custom** mark, and then choose a mark from the available symbols. This will not change the existing note reference marks. It will only add new ones.

EndNote

6.5.2 Change the number format of footnotes or endnotes

Place the insertion point in the section in which someone want to change the footnote or endnote format. If the document is not divided into sections, place the insertion point anywhere in the document.

☐ On the **References** tab, click the **Footnote & Endnote Dialog Box Launcher**.

☐ Click **Footnotes** or **Endnotes**

☐ In the **Number** format box, click the option that someone want.

☐ Click **Apply**.

6.5.3 Change the starting value for footnotes or endnotes

Word will automatically number footnotes beginning with "1" and endnotes beginning with "i", or someone can choose a different starting value.

NOTE If the footnotes in the document are numbered incorrectly, the document may contain tracked changes. Accept the tracked changes so that Word will correctly number the footnotes and endnotes.

☐ On the References tab, in the Footnotes group, click the **Footnote & Endnote Dialog Box Launcher**

☐ In the Start at box, choose the desired starting value.

☐ Click **Apply**.

6.5.4 Create a footnote or endnote continuation notice

If a footnote or endnote is too long to fit on a page, someone can create a continuation notice to let readers know that a footnote or endnote is continued on the next page.

☐ Make sure that someone are in **Draft** view by going to the **View** tab and clicking **Draft**.

☐ On the **References** tab, in the **Footnotes** group, click **Show Notes**.

☐ If the document contains both footnotes and endnotes, a message appears. Click **View footnote** area or **View endnote** area, and then click **OK**.

☐ In the note pane list, click **Footnote Continuation Notice** or **Endnote Continuation Notice**.

☐ In the **note pane**, type the text that someone want to use for the continuation notice.

6.5.5 Change or remove a footnote or endnote separator

Word separates document text from footnotes and endnotes with a short horizontal line called a note separator. If a note overflows onto the next page, Word prints a longer line called a note continuation separator. Someone can customize separators by adding text or graphics.

☐ In the note **pane** list, click and choose the type of separator someone want to change or remove.

☐ To change the separator that appears between the document text and notes, click **Footnote Separator** or **Endnote Separator**.

☐ To change the separator for notes that continue from the previous page, click **Footnote Continuation Separator** or **Endnote Continuation Separator**.

☐ Select the separator and make changes:

☐ To remove the separator, press **DELETE**.

☐ To edit the separator, insert a Clip Art divider line or type text.

☐ To restore the default separator, click **Reset**.

6.5.6 Delete a footnote or an endnote

When someone want to delete a note, someone work with the note reference mark in the document window, not the text in the note.

If someone delete an automatically numbered note reference mark, Word renumbers the notes in the new order.

Delete a note

In the document, select the note reference mark of the footnote or endnote that someone want to delete, and then press DELETE.

6.6 PRINT DOCUMENT

On the Print tab, the properties for the default printer automatically appear in the first section, and the preview of the document automatically appears in the second section.

Click the **File** tab, and then click **Print**.

Tip: To go back to the document and make changes before someone print it, click the **File** tab.

☐ When the properties for the printer and document appear the way that someone want them to, click **Print**.

Note: To change the properties for the printer, under the printer name, click **Printer Properties**.

6.6.1 Print on both sides of the paper (duplex printing) in Word

Some printers offer the option of automatically printing on both sides of a sheet of paper (automatic duplex printing). Other printers provide instructions so that someone can manually reinsert pages to print the second side (manual duplex printing). Some printers do not support duplex printing at all.

Find out whether the printer supports automatic duplex printing

To check whether the printer supports duplex printing, someone can check the printer manual or consult the printer manufacturer, or someone can do the following:

☐ Click the **File** tab.

☐ Click **Print**.

☐ Under **Settings**, click **Print One Sided**. If Print on **Both Sides** is available, the printer is set up for **duplex** printing.

Office

Notes:

☐ If someone are printing to a combination copy machine and printer, and the copy machine supports two-sided copying, it probably supports automatic duplex printing.

☐ If someone have more than one printer installed, it is possible that one printer supports duplex printing and another printer does not.

Set up a printer to print to both sides of a sheet of paper

If the printer doesn't support automatic duplex printing, someone have two other options. Someone can use manual duplex printing, or someone can print the odd and even pages separately.

Print by using manual duplex

If the printer does not support automatic duplex printing, someone can print all of the pages that appear on one side of the paper and then, after someone are prompted, turn the stack over and feed the pages into the printer again.

In Word, do the following:

☐ Click the **File** tab.

☐ Click **Print**.

☐ Under **Settings**, click **Print One Sided**, and then click **Manually Print on Both Sides**.

When someone print, Word will prompt someone to turn over the stack to feed the pages into the printer again.

6.6.2 Print odd and even pages

Someone can also use the following procedure to print on both sides:

☐ Click the **File** tab.

☐ Click **Print**.

☐ Under **Settings**, click **Print All Pages**. Near the bottom of the gallery, click **Only Print Odd Pages**.

☐ Click the **Print button** at the top of the gallery.

☐ After the odd pages are printed, flip the stack of pages over, and then under **Settings**, click **Print All Pages**. At the bottom of the gallery, click **Only Print Even Pages**.

☐ Click the **Print** button at the top of the gallery.

Note: *Depending on the printer model, someone might have to rotate and reorder the pages to print the other side of the stack.*

6.7 SUMMARY

In this chapter we have discussed all about printing and setting word document.

Microsoft Word places all the page setup controls in one convenient place, the aptly

titled Page Setup dialog box, so someone can make all the changes in one fell swoop.

These are just some of the options someone can change in the Page Setup dialog box, but if someone master these, someone are well on the way to producing professional quality work and displaying the word processing prowess.

We have discussed about various views of the word document, such as normal, draft

outline, document map, reading, full screen.

Word offers someone several options to change the presentation of the text such as to put the text in bold, in italic or in underlined. It's also possible to change the font as well as cuts it letters and its colors from the others. The pagination allows someone to control the options of presentation of the document on paper. Someone can change the margins, the size(format) of the paper, the orientation of the paper and the other options that will be explained lower on this page.

Add page numbers and headers and footers by using the gallery, or create a custom

page number, header, or footer.

For best results, decide first whether someone want only a page number or whether someone wants information plus a page number in the header or footer. If someone want a page number and no other information, add a page number. If someone want a page number plus other information, or if someone just want the other information, add a header or footer.

Footnotes and endnotes are used in printed documents to explain, comment on, or

provide references for text in a document. Someone might use footnotes for detailed

comments and endnotes for citation of sources. A footnote or an endnote consists of

two linked parts — the note reference mark and the corresponding note text. On the

Print tab, the properties for the default printer automatically appear in the first section,

and the preview of the document automatically appears in the second section.

Chapter 7

Introduction to Mail Merge, Macros and Charts

7.1 INTRODUCTION

Microsoft word 2016 offers the advanced word processing functions namely:

1. Mail Merge

2. Macros and

3. Graphs/ Charts

Someone use mail merge when someone want to create a set of documents, such as a form letter that is sent to many customers or a sheet of address labels. Each letter or label has the same kind of information, yet the content is unique. For example, in letters to the customers, each letter can be personalized to address each customer by name. The unique information in each letter or label comes from entries in a data source.

The mail merge process entails the following overall steps:

1. Set up the main document. The main document contains the text and graphics that are the same for each version of the merged document. For example, the return address or salutation in a form letter.

2. Connect the document to a data source. A data source is a file that contains the information to be merged into a document. For example, the names and addresses of the recipients of a letter.

3. Refine the list of recipients or Microsoft Office Word generates a copy of the main document for each item, or record, in the data file. If the data file is a mailing list, these items are probably recipients of the mailing. If someone want to generate copies for only certain items in the data file, someone can choose which records to include.

4. Add placeholders, called mail merge fields, to the document. When someone perform the mail merge, the mail merge fields are filled with information from the data file.

5. Preview and complete the merge. Someone can preview each copy of the document before someone print the whole set.

Someone use commands on the Mailings tab to perform a mail merge.

In Microsoft Office Word, someone can automate frequently used tasks by creating macros. A macro is a series of commands and instructions that someone group together as a single command to accomplish a task automatically.

Typical uses for macros are:

1. To speed up routine editing and formatting

2. To combine multiple commands — for example, to insert a table with a specific size and borders, and with a specific number of rows and columns

3. To make an option in a dialog box more accessible

4. To automate a complex series of tasks

Someone can use the macro recorder to record a sequence of actions, or someone can create a macro from scratch by entering Visual Basic for Applications (Visual Basic for Applications (VBA): A macro-language version of Microsoft Visual Basic that is used to program Microsoft Windows-based applications and is included with several Microsoft program code in the Visual Basic Editor (Visual Basic Editor: An environment in which someone write new and edit existing Visual Basic for Applications code and procedures. The Visual Basic Editor contains a complete debugging toolset for finding syntax, run-time, and logic problem in the code.).

Office Word 2016 includes many different types of charts and graphs that someone can use to inform the audience about inventory levels, organizational changes, sales figures, and much more. Charts are fully integrated with Office Word 2016. When someone have Excel installed, someone can create Excel charts in Word by clicking the Chart button on the Ribbon (Insert tab, Illustrations group), and then by using the chart tools to modify or format the chart. Charts that someone create will be embedded in Office Word 2016, and the chart data is stored in an Excel worksheet that is incorporated in the Word file.

Note If someone work in Compatibility Mode in Word, someone can insert a chart by using Microsoft Graph instead of Excel.

Someone can also copy a chart from Excel to Office Word 2016. When someone copy a chart, it can either be embedded as static data or linked to the workbook. For a chart that is linked to a workbook that someone have access to, someone can specify that it automatically check for changes in the linked workbook whenever the chart is opened.

Someone can add a chart or graph to the document in one of two ways:

☐ **Someone can insert a chart in the document by embedding** (embedded object: Information (object) contained in a source file and inserted into a destination file. Once embedded, the object becomes part of the destination file. Changes someone make to the embedded object are reflected in the destination file.) it When someone embeds data from an Excel chart in Word, someone edit that data in Office Excel 2016, and the worksheet is saved with the Word document.

☐ **Someone can paste an Excel chart into the presentation and link to data in Office Excel 2016** When someone copy a chart from Office Excel 2016 and paste it into the document, the data in the chart is linked to the Excel worksheet. The Excel worksheet is a separate file and is not saved with the Word document.

In this case, because the Excel worksheet is not part of the Word document, if someone wants to change the data in the chart, someone must make the changes to the linked worksheet in Office Excel 2016.

7.2 MAIL MERGE

Mail merge techniques allow someone to create a document which combines repetitive text elements with data drawn from an external data document. To perform mail merge, someone'll need the following:

☐ A template (previously created, or generated during the merge)

☐ A recipient list or data source (created during the merge. or an existing file)

Word will then create a new document by inserting the data from the data source into the structure of the template document.

On the **Mailings** tab, click **Start Mail Merge**, and then click **Step by Step Mail Merge Wizard**.

Select document type

1. In the **Mail Merge** task pane, click **Letters**. This will allow someone to send letters to a group of people and personalize the results of the letter that each person receives.

2. Click **Next: Starting document**.

Select the starting document

1. Click one of the following options:

- **Use the current document**: Use the currently open document as the main document.

- **Start from a template**: Select one of the ready-to-use mail merge templates.

- **Start from existing document**: Open an existing document to use as the mail merge main document.

2. In the **Mail Merge** task pane, click **Next: Select recipients**.

Select recipients

When someone open or create a data source by using the Mail Merge Wizard, someone are telling Word to use a specific set of variable information for the merge. Use one of the following methods to attach the main document to the data source.

Method 1: Use an existing data source

To use an existing data source, follow these steps:

1. In the **Mail Merge** task pane, click **Use an existing list**.

2. In the **Use an existing list** section, click **Browse**.

3. In the **Select Data Source** dialog box, select the file that contains the variable information that someone want to use, and then click **Open**.

Note: *If the data source is not listed in the list of files, select the appropriate drive and folder. If necessary, select the appropriate option in the All Data Sources list. Select the file, and then click Open.*

Word displays the **Mail Merge Recipients** dialog box. Someone can sort and edit the data if someone want to.

4. Click **OK** to return to the main document.

5. Save the main document.

When someone save the main document at this point, someone are also saving the data source and attaching the data source to the main document

6. Type the name that someone want to give to the main document, and then

click **Save**.

Method 2: Use names from a Microsoft Outlook Contacts List

To use an Outlook Contact List, follow these steps:

1. In the Mail Merge task pane, click **Next: Select recipients**.

2. Click **Select from Outlook contacts**.

3. In the **Select from Outlook contacts** section, click **Choose Contacts Folder**.

4. In the **Select Contact List Folder** dialog box, select the Outlook contacts folder that someone want, and then click **OK**.

Word displays the **Mail Merge Recipients** dialog box. Someone can sort and edit the data if someone want.

5. Click **OK** to return to the main document.

Method 3: Create a database of names and addresses

To create a new database, follow these steps:

1. In the Mail Merge task pane, click **Next: Select Recipients**.

2. Click **Type a new list**.

3. Click **Create**.

The **New Address List** dialog box appears. In this dialog box, enter the address information for each record. If there is no information for a particular field, leave the box blank.

By default, Word skips blank fields. Therefore, the merge is not affected if blank entries are in the data form. The set of information in each form makes up one data record.

4. After someone type the information for a record, click **New Entry** to move to the next record.

To delete a record, click **Delete Entry**. To search for a specific record, click **Find Entry**. To customize the list, click **Customize**. In the **Customize Address List** dialog box, someone can add, delete, rename, and reorder the merge fields.

5. In the **New Address List** dialog box, click **OK**. In the **Save Address**

List dialog box, type the name that someone want to give to the data source in the **File name** box, and then click **Save**.

6. In the **Mail Merge Recipients** dialog box, make any changes that someone want, and then click **OK**.

7. Click **Next: Write the letter** to finish setting up the letter.

8. Save the main document.

When someone save the main document at this point, someone are also saving the data source and attaching the data source to the main document.

9. Type the name that someone want to give to the main document, and then click **Save**.

To proceed to the next step, click **Next: Write the letter**.

Write the letter

In this step, someone set up the main document.

☐ Type or add any text and graphics that someone want to include in the letter.

☐ Add the field codes where someone want the variable information to appear. In the **Mail Merge** task pane, someone have four options:

o **Address block**: Use this option to insert a formatted address.

o **Greeting line**: Use this option to insert a formatted salutation.

o **Electronic postage**: Use this option to insert electronic postage.

Note: This option requires that someone have a postage software program installed on the computer.

o **More Items** Use this option to insert individual merge fields. When someone click **More Items,** the **Insert Merge Field** dialog box appears.

Note: Make sure that the cursor is where someone want to insert the information from the data source before someone click More Items.

o In the **Insert Merge Field** dialog box, click the merge field that someone want to use, and then click **Insert**.

*Note: Someone can insert all of the fields and then go back and add any spaces or punctuation. Alternatively, someone can insert one field at a time, close the **Insert Merge Fields** dialog box, add any spaces or punctuation that someone want, and then repeat this step for each additional merge field that someone want to insert. Someone can also format* *(apply bold or italic formatting to) the merge fields, just like regular text.*

☐ When someone finish editing the main document, click **Save** or **Save As** on the **File** menu.

Note*: In Word 2016, click the **Microsoft Office Button**, and then click **Save** or **Save As**.*

Name the file, and then click **Save**. To proceed to the next step, click **Next: Preview the letters**.

Preview the letters

This step allows someone to preview the merged data, one letter at a time. Someone can also make changes to the recipient list or personalize individual letters.

To proceed to the next step, click **Next: Complete the merge**.

Complete the merge

This step merges the variable information with the form letter. Someone can output the merge result by using either of the following options:

☐ **Print**: Select this option to send the merged document directly to the printer. Someone will not be able to view the document on the screen.

When someone click **Print**, the **Merge to Printer** dialog box appears. In the **Merge to Printer** dialog box, someone can choose which records to merge. When someone click **OK**, the **Print** dialog box appears. Click **Print** to print the merge document.

☐ **Edit individual letters**: Select this option to display the merged document on the screen.

When someone click **Edit individual letters**, the **Merge to New Document** dialog box appears. In the **Merge to New Document** dialog box, someone can choose which records to merge. When someone click **OK**, the documents are merged to a new Word document.

To print the file, on the **File** menu, click **Print**.

Note In Word 2016, click the **Microsoft Office Button**, and then click **Print**.

Additional resources

For troubleshooting, see the Word Mail Merge Support Resources. To do this, visit the following Microsoft Web site: http://support.microsoft.com/wd2002mailmerge

Glossary

□ **Address list**: An address list is a file that contains the data that varies in each copy of a merged document. For example, a data source can include the name and address of each recipient of a form letter.

□ **Boilerplate**: Generic information that is repeated in each form letter, mailing label, envelope, or directory (catalog).

□ **Data field**: A category of information in a data source. A data fields corresponds to one column of information in the data source. The name of each data field is listed in the first row (header row) of the data source. "PostalCode" and "LastName" are examples of data field names.

□ **Data record**: A complete set of related information in a data source. A data record corresponds to one row of information in the data source. All information about one client in a client mailing list is an example of a data record.

□ **Delimited file**: A text file that has data fields separated (or delimited) by tab characters or commas, and data records delimited by paragraph marks.

□ **Header row**: The first row (or record) in a mail merge data source. The header row contains the field names for the categories of information in the data source; for example, "Name" and "City." The header row can also be stored in a separate document called the header source.

□ **Main document**: In a mail merge operation, the document that contains the text and graphics that remain the same for each version of the merged document; for example, the return address and body of a form letter.

□ **Merge field**: A placeholder that someone insert in the main document. Merge fields tell Microsoft Word where to insert specific information from the data source. For example, insert the merge field "City" to have Word insert a city name, such as "Paris," that is stored in the City data field

□ **Merged document**: The document that is created by merging the data from the data source into the main document.

7.3 MACROS

A macro is typically a series of commands or instructions that are combined to form a single command. Macros can save someone time by letting someone automate relatively simple tasks that someone need to perform often, as well as complex procedures that consist of many steps. Macros can be powerful tools that can greatly reduce the time that someone will need to finish the work and can eliminate the need to remember all the steps in a tedious procedure. Even if someone know nothing about writing macros, someone can create macros by using the Macro Recorder, which records the steps that someone perform and translates them into macro code.

Everyone can use macros. Someone do not need any programming knowledge to use macros, and someone can obtain macros without ever writing any code theself. The macros that can help someone do the work faster and easier can be obtained and installed in several ways, including the following.

☐ Macros can be created by using the Macro Recorder, which records the steps that someone perform and translates them into macro code.

☐ If someone can verbally describe what someone want a macro to do, someone can post a request to the Microsoft Office Customization and Programming forum, and one or more of the experts who will read the request will be happy to write the macro for someone.

☐ The code of a macro can be copied as text from a reliable trustworthy source and added to the **New Macros** module of a template, from which it will always be available.

☐ Macros that are stored in a template that someone obtain from a reliable trustworthy source can be made available by installing the template or by using the Organizer to copy the applicable module into an installed template.

Recording a Macro and Assigning a Keyboard Shortcut to It

To see how to record a macro and use it, consider the scenario in which someone type two letters in the wrong order without creating a spelling error, as in the case of typing the word for instead of the word for. One way to fix this error is to press Backspace twice and retype the correct letters. That solution requires four keystrokes, but the same correction can be done in one keystroke with a recorded macro assigned to a keyboard shortcut.

Because a macro does not automatically remember the characters that are deleted when someone press Backspace twice, when we record the macro, we will cut the second of the characters that were typed in the wrong order, place the cursor before the first of the characters that were typed in the wrong order, and insert the character that we copied to the clipboard in that position as described in the following procedure.

To record a macro and assign a shortcut key to it

☐ Type the word fro.

☐ Start the Macro Recorder.

☐ To do this in Word 2010 or Word 2016, on the **View** tab, click the lower part of the **Macros**botton, and then click **Record Macro**.

☐ Alternatively, in Word 2010 or Word 2016, someone can also start the macro recorder from the **Developer** tab. To start the macro recorder from the **Developer** tab, in the **Code** group, click **Record Macro**.

☐ If someone is using Word 2010 and the **Developer** tab is not shown, on the **File** tab, click **Options**. Then in the **Word Options** dialog box, click **Customize Ribbon**, under **Customize the Ribbon** select the **Developer** check box and click **OK**.

☐ If someone is using Word 2016 and the **Developer** tab is not shown, click the Microsoft Office Button, click **Word Options**, click **Popular**, and under **Top options for working with Word**, select the **Show Developer tab in the Ribbon** check box.

To do this in Word 2003, on the **Tools** menu, point to **Macro**, and then click **Record New Macro**.

☐ In the **Record Macro** dialog box, in the **Macro name** box, replace the default name of the macro by a meaningful name, such as Reverse Letters.

☐ Click the **Keyboard** button

☐ In the **Commands** box, verify that the name of the macro that someone are creating is selected.

☐ In the **Press new shortcut key** box, press **Shift+Backspace** or a different key or press key sequence that someone want to use, and then click **Assign**.

☐ In the **Store macro in** box, leave the default setting.

☐ Click **Close** to start recording the macro.

☐ Press **Shift+Left**.

☐ Press **Ctrl+X**.

☐ Press **Left**.

☐ Press **Ctrl+V**.

☐ Press **Right**.

Stop the recording of the macro.

☐ To do this in Word 2010 or Word 2016, on the **View** tab, click the lower part of the **Macros**botton, and then click **Stop Recording**.

☐ Alternatively, in Word 2010 or Word 2016, on the **Developer** tab, in the **Code** group, click **Stop Recording**.

To do this in Word 2003, on the **Stop Recording** toolbar, click the **Stop Recording** button ( ).

The new macro is now ready to use at any time by pressing **Shift+Backspace**. Someone can test it by reversing any two letters as someone type any word, stopping after the reversed letters, and pressing **Shift+Backspace**. Someone can now press **Shift+Backspace** anywhere in a document to switch the order of the last two characters before the cursor.

Note. If the name that someone assign to a macro is identical to the name of a built-in Word command, the actions defined in the macro will replace the actions of the built-in Word command. To view a list of the names of the built-in Word commands, press **Alt+F8**, and in the **Macros in** drop-down list, select **Word Commands**.

Modifying an Existing Macro

The recorded version of the ReverseLetters macro uses the clipboard to store a letter. If someone do not want the ReverseLetters macro to change the clipboard contents, someon can replace the recorded version of this macro by the following manually revised version, which copies the second of the characters that were typed in the wrong order to a String variable instead of the clipboard.

Sub ReverseLetters()

' Macro that reverses the order of the last two

characters

```
' before the cursor.
Dim myChar As String
Selection.MoveLeft Unit:=wdCharacter, Count:=1,
Extend:=wdExtend
myChar = Selection.Text
Selection.Delete
Selection.MoveLeft Unit:=wdCharacter, Count:=1
Selection.TypeText myChar
Selection.MoveRight Unit:=wdCharacter, Count:=1
End Sub
```

Someone can use the following procedure for modifying an existing macro that is stored in the default global template to replace the recorded version of the ReverseLetters macro by the manually revised version.

To replace the code of an existing macro by a revised version

☐ In the browser, select the code of the revised version of the macro after the first line, which contains the word Sub and the name of the macro, to end of the line containing End Sub, and then press **Ctrl+C**.

Note that the first line of the macro is not copied together with the rest of the macro because replacing this line in the recorded macro would delete the keyboard shortcut that someone defined.

☐ In any Word document, press **Alt+F8**.

☐ In the **Macros** dialog box, under **Macro name**, select the name of the macro that someone want to modify and click **Edit**.

☐ In the Visual Basic Editor, select the code of the macro after the first line, which contains the wordSub and the name of the macro, to end of the line containing End Sub.

☐ Press **Ctrl+V**.

☐ Press **Ctrl+S** to save the changes and close (or minimize) the Visual Basic Editor.

It should be mentioned here that a macro may contain code which instructs Word to repeat an action until a certain condition is met. Such code is called a *loop*. If the circuMicrosofttances are such that the condition is never fulfilled, Word will continue to execute the code within the loop indefinitely and will appear to hang. If Word appears to hang while someone are running a macro, someone can stop the execution of the macro by pressingCtrl+Break and then clicking **End**.

Renaming, Deleting, and Copying Macros

As someone continue to use macros, someone may want to rename a macro, delete a macro, or copy macros to a template. The following procedures describe the steps needed to perform these tasks.

To rename a macro

☐ In any Word document, press Alt+F8.

☐ In the **Macros** dialog box, in the **Macros in** drop-down list, select the applicable template or document.

☐ In the **Macro name** box, select the name of the macro that someone want to change and click **Edit**.

☐ In the Visual Basic Editor, in the first line of the macro, which begins with the word Sub, change the existing name to the new name, but do not remove the word Sub or the pair of parentheses at the end of the line.

☐ Press Ctrl+S to save the changes and close (or minimize) the Visual Basic Editor.

To delete a macro

☐ In any Word document, press Alt+F8.

☐ In the **Macros** dialog box, in the **Macros in** drop-down list, select the applicable template or document.

☐ In the **Macro name** box, select the name of the macro that someone want to delete.

☐ Click **Delete**.

By default, the macros that someone create in Word are stored in the NewMacros module of the default global template, which is Normal.dotm in Word 2016 or Normal.dot in earlier versions of Word. Macros can be stored in a template or in a document. Macros stored in the default global template are always available and can be run from any document. Macros stored in a document are available only when the document is active. To distribute macros to other users, copy the module containing them to a template that someone created, distribute the template file, and instruct them to install the template in their templates folder. The macros will be available whenever a document based the template is the active document. Alternatively, someone can instruct them to install the template in the Word Startup folder. To determine the location of these folders in Word 2016, click the Microsoft Office Button, click **Word Options**, click **Advanced**, scroll down to the **General** section, and click **File Locations**. In Word 2003, on the **Tools** menu, click **Options**, and then in the **Options** dialog box, click the **File Locations** tab. A template that is stored in the Word Startup folder is a global template or an add-in. The macros in templates that are in the Word Startup folder can be called from any document.

7.4 GRAPHS / CHARTS

Graphs and charts help readers understand complex figures by presenting those numbers in a concise, visual format. Effective graphs work in conjunction with the narrative and can be dynamic presentation tools. If someone want to learn how to add a graph to Microsoft Word, follow these guidelines.

7.4.1 Steps   1.

Determine where someone want to insert a graph into the text. Someone wants the graph adjacent to the section of the corresponding narrative. This allows the reader to easily scan the graph and search the accompanying type for further details. Ideally, the cogent text will wrap around the chart.

2. **Insert a graph inside the Word document.** Set the cursor inside the section of text that corresponds to the graph someone'll be adding.

☐ At the top of the document, click the "Insert" menu.

☐ Find the "Object" menu on the right side of the toolbar and click it.

Introduction to Mail Merge, Macros and Charts / 179

☐ A new Object window will open. Under the "Create New ☐" tab, scroll down to Microsoft Graph Chart. Make sure it is highlighted, and click "OK."

3. **Turn an Excel Spreadsheet into a Microsoft Graph Chart.** If someone want to turn a spreadsheet into a chart someone can use inside a Word document, the process is simple.

☐ Select the Excel Spreadsheet so that it is highlighted and copy it by clicking

"Ctrl+C." Mac users click "Cmmd+C."

☐ In the Word document, click where someone want the chart to appear.

☐ Paste the spreadsheet into the document by holding down the Ctrl key and hitting "V."

☐ With the cursor next to the data, click "Paste Options." To input the spreadsheet as a Word table, click "Keep Source Formatting." The chart will look like it did in Excel. Click "Match Destination Table Style" if someone want the new graph to look like others someone are using in the document.

4. Manipulate data inside the chart someone created. The sample graph in most editions of Microsoft Word lists quarterly figures for 3 different entities: East, North and West. Changing data inside a Microsoft Graph Chart can be done easily.

☐ **Change figures**: To change the numbers in a Microsoft Graph Chart, simply click inside the appropriate cell and make sure it contains a bold border. Type in the new numbers and hit Enter. Both the figure and the bar on the graph will change.

☐ **Change keys:** To change the information in the chart's key, click the cell someone want to update and type in the new information. The new name someone typed in will have a corresponding color.

☐ **Add item:** If someone need to expand the number of entries in the chart, type a name into the next cell under the current names and hit "Enter." The new entry automatically is added to the graph key and gets a color-coded bar. Add the entry's figures in the appropriate cells to complete the graph.

☐ **Delete item:** To delete an entire row in a Microsoft Graph Chart, click on the number at the left of the datasheet and press "Delete" on the keyboard. To delete a column, click on the corresponding letter at the top of the chart and click the "Delete" key.

☐ **Change bar colors:** Place the cursor over the bar someone want to change and double-click it. The Format Data Series window will open with a complete color palette. Select the new color someone want and click "OK." Someone also can change the shape of the bars and the spacing between them from in this window.

5. Adjust the chart position and dimensions: Word automatically changes the proportions of the graph based on the changes someone make. Moving a graph within text can be done 1 of 2 ways:

☐ **Moving a graph manually:** Click on the graph. To change the height or width of the chart, move the cursor over 1 of its 8 sizing dots. When the cursor changes to a pointer, drag the cursor in the direction someone want to resize the chart. A marquee will appear. When someone is satisfied with the new shape, release and the chart will be resized proportionally.

☐ **Positioning a graph automatically:** From the Page Lay out menu, click the chart. Go to Position and select the option someone desire. As someone roll the cursor over each presentation, the graph will change position inside the document to give someone a preview of how it will look. By clicking a particular option, someone set the chart position inside the text.

☐ **Wrapping text around a graph:** To wrap text around a chart, select the graph from the Page Layout menu. From the Position dropdown, select More Lay out Options. The Lay out window will open. Choose the "Text Wrapping" tab and input the values for the Distance around Text

7.4.2 Create a chart from a Word table

1. Create a table in Word, with text labels in the top row and left column, and numbers in other cells.

2. Click in the table.

3. On the **Table** menu, point to **Select**, and then click **Table**.

4. On the **Insert** menu, click **Object**, and then click the **Create New** tab.

5. In the **Object** type box, double-click **Microsoft Graph** Chart.

Word displays a chart with the information from the table someone created. The data associated with the chart is in a table called a datasheet.

Someone can edit the data in the chart by clicking a cell on the datasheet andrevising the entry.

6. To return to **Word**, click the **Word** document.

7.4.3 Change the chart to another chart type

Use these steps to change the chart to another chart type, such as a pie chart or a bar

chart.

1. On the **Chart** menu, click **Chart** Type.

2. Choose a chart type from the options on the **Standard** Types and **Custom**

Types tabs.

7.4.4 Get Help about charts/ Graphs

For more information about working with charts — for example, how to add data

labels, change the scale of the value axis, or troubleshoot charts — use the following

procedure to see Microsoft Excel Help or Microsoft Graph Help. To work with charts

created in Graph or Excel, someone must have Graph or Excel installed.

1. In **Word**, double-click the chart.

2. The **menus** and **toolbars** change to show the **Graph** or Excel menus and

buttons.

3. On the **Help** menu, click **Microsoft Graph Help** or **Microsoft Excel Help**.

7.5 SUMMARY

In this chapter we have discussed about the step by step method of using Mail merge,

Macros and Graphs/charts in word.

Mail merge techniques allow someone to create a document which combines repetitive text elements with data drawn from an external data document. To perform mail merge,

someone'll need the following:

☐ A template (previously created, or generated during the merge)

☐ A recipient list or data source (created during the merge. or an existing file)

Word will then create a new document by inserting the data from the data source into

the structure of the template document. A macro is typically a series of commands or instructions that are combined to form a single command. Macros can save someone time by letting someone automate relatively simple tasks that someone need to perform often, as well as complex procedures that consist of many steps. Macros can be powerful tools that can greatly reduce the time that someone will need to finish the work and can eliminate the need to remember all the steps in a tedious procedure. Even if someone know nothing about writing macros, someone can create macros by using the Macro Recorder, which records the steps that someone perform and translates them into macro code. Graphs and charts help readers understand complex figures by presenting those

numbers in a concise, visual format. Effective graphs work in conjunction with the

narrative and can be dynamic presentation tools. If someone want to learn how to add a

graph to Microsoft Word, follow these guidelines.

Chapter 8

8.1 INTRODUCTION

Excel is one of the very advanced program of Microsoft Office with the help
of which someone can perform analysis of complex inter related columnar reports in
workspaces called as **worksheets** or **spreadsheets.** Worksheets are made up of
cells with array of rows and columns. Excel rows are generally identified with
numbers and the columns are identified with letters. The address of each cell is its
row and column label. eg. cell C8 would be the cell in the Cth i.e. third column
and 8th row. Someone can also create formulas called as **equations** in cells. A number
of formatting features are available to present the work in an attractive manner. A
Chart Wizard helps someone to convert the data in the worksheet into pie charts, line
graphs, bar charts, 3-D charts, etc.

Remember that many of the formatting features offered by Windows can be used
in Excel in the same manner. Many commands are located in the same menus as they
are in Word. It is also easy to paste Excel data into Word or PowerPoint documents.
Let us now start off with our study of Excel basics.

8.2 CREATING A WORKSHEET

Start the Excel program. Someone can open the Excel program from the Start submenu
or click on the Excel shortcut on the desktop (if it is present). The worksheet will open.

Someone can use the PageSetup command from the Excel's file menu for setting the page
size, orientation, header and footer dimensions etc. In the beginning, while learning

Excel it would be a good idea to use the default settings of Excel. As someone become an
expert in using Excel, someone can set up the own pages as per the requirements. When
someone open Excel the worksheet it will appear as follows:

The Title bar displays the name of the current workbook open.

The Menu bar is used to access the menus from which someone select the various
Excel commands.

The Standard toolbar displays the buttons which someone can use to perform the
commonly needed tasks.

The Formatting toolbar displays buttons and lists that can be used to change the appearance of the data.

The reference area displays information about the current workbook cell. The Formula bar is used to enter and edit data.

The cells are areas where someone place data and formulas. The active cell is indicated by a black outline.

The row heading and column heading help to identify cells.

The status bar displays information about the status of Excel and the system.

8.2.1 Selecting cells:

Before entering or editing cell contents or before formatting or moving cells, they must be selected. Someone can select cells with the help of keyboard or mouse. Remember someone

can select a single cell or a group of cells.

Selecting cells with a Mouse:

• Click on a row number to select the whole row

• Point to the column's heading to select the entire column

• Click and drag to select a specific range of cells.

• Click on the empty button at the top left corner of the workbook to select the entire worksheet.

• If someone wish to select noncontiguous cells or group of cells, hold down the Ctrl key and select.

Selecting cells with a keyboard:

If someone has already selected a range of cells, press Shift+Spacebar to select the entire row or rows in which the cells are located.

To select entire column press Ctrl+ Spacebar

Ctrl+Shift+Spacebar will **select the entire worksheet.**

In order to extend selections, in any direction someone can hold down the Shift key and press the appropriate arrow key.]

Formula Bar

Tool Ribbon

Menu Ba

Cell Reference

Selected Cell

8.3 ENTERING AND EDITING TEXT

To enter the text in the worksheet, someone should activate the cell where someone wish to insert the text. Someone can activate a cell by pointing to it and clicking it. As soon as the cell is activated, someone can begin typing. As someone start typing, the text will appear in the active cell, as well as in the Formula bar. When someone press Enter, the text entry will be complete, and the text will be placed in the active cell. Press the Esc key to cancel the text entry.

Someone can type up to 255 characters per cell.

Editing Text:

The Windows text editing features can be used to edit the text in the cells. If someone wish to edit an entry in a cell simply activate the cell and edit as someone would normally do with Windows commands.

Replacing Text: To replace a text, simply activate a cell then type the new text and press Enter. The new text will replace the old text in the activated cell. Someone can make use of the buttons in the Formatting tool bar to make the text bold, change the Font, etc. The Format menu can also be used for additional choices of formatting.

Text Boxes: Someone can also create text boxes and place them anywhere someone want in the worksheet. To create a text box, click the Text Box button. Someone make use of the mouse to drag a box of the desired size. Someone can type the text in the box. It is also possible to rotate text in text boxes.

Comments (Text Notes): Comments are used to hold notes which someone do not wish to display on the worksheets. These notes are attached to the cells and can be viewed on screen. To create a comment, select the appropriate cell and then choose insert Comment or press Shift + F2. A red dot appears in the top right corner of the cell indicating that a note has been attached to this cell. Type the note and press Enter.

The note gets attached to the cell. If someone wish to display the note, select the cell and press Shift+F2. Someone can also print comments. For this purpose, open the Page Setup

Dialog box, click on the Sheet tab and select the Comment option box.

Undo and Repeat Commands: The Edit menu contains the Undo and Repeat commands similar to those of Word. The Undo and Redo buttons are also available on the Standard toolbar.

Entering and Formatting Numbers:

Numbers are often referred to as **values** in Excel. In addition to numbers someone can also enter the following symbols when typing numbers:

+ - ( ) , . $ % E e

Excel ignores the + sign in numeric entries. If someone precede a number with the -(minus) sign the number is considered to be negative. Excel also accepts numbers in the scientific notation eg. 1.3E+5. When someone enter dollar signs, percentages or commas, Excel changes the format of the number.

If a number is too big to be properly displayed in its cell, Excel often displays a series of pound signs (#######) instead of the number. At other times, Excel shifts to the scientific notation to display the number. Of course, someone can make the column wider or use a shorter number format to overcome this situation.

Entering and Formatting Dates and Times:

Some of the common date and time formats are:

14/9/05

13-Sep-03

Sep 13, 2003

3:15 PM

3:15:26 PM

15:15:26

13/9/03 15:15

Someone can also create the own date formats.

Treating numbers as Text : Sometimes someone may want Excel to treat numbers, time entries or date like entries as text instead of numbers. In such a situation, precede the entry with a (single quotation mark). This mark is not displayed or printed, but the number entered after it would be treated as text entries.

8.4 FORMULAS

Formulas are created when someone wish to add columns of numbers, divide one number by another, and such other computations. Usually, someone will place the formula in the cell where someone wish to see the result. The formula is typed in the Formula bar. The formula should start with the = sign. (The & sign can also be used).

8.4.1 To create a formula:

- Activate the cell where someone wish to place the formula.

- Type the equal sign or the ampersand (&). This will tell Excel that someone wish to create a formula.

- Then type the formula eg. If someone has activated cell C10 and wish to place contents of C8+C9 into C10 then, type =C8 + C9 and press Enter. If someone has entered values in C8 and C9, then they will be added, and the sum will appear in cell C10.

8.4.2 Formula operators:

Excel operators are divided into four general categories: arithmetic, comparison, text and reference. Arithmetic operators are the most commonly used.

The standard arithmetic operators are:

+ Addition - Subtraction

* Multiplication / Division

% Percentage ^ Exponentiation

Someone can also make use of parenthesis along with these operators.

Comparison Operators: The comparison operators are :

= Equal <> Not equal to

>> Greater than >>= Greater than or equal to

<< Less than <<= Less than or equal to

8.4.3 Text operator: The only text operator in Excel is the ampersand (&). It

is used to combine text. eg. If someone have the text "Good" in cell A10 and the text "Morning" in cell A11 then, the formula =A10 & A11 would create the text string "GoodMorning".

8.4.4 Reference operators : Excel offers reference operators. The most common

reference is to a range of cells. eg. A1:C15 refers to cells A1, C15 and all cells in between them. We shall study ranges later.

8.4.5 Referencing Cells: In many situations when creating formulas, someone may be required to refer to a single cell only. A single cell reference refers to a specific cell. At other times someone may be required to refer to range of cells eg. (C3 to C7 in the following example to find sum total of English subject.) Someone can specify references by clicking or dragging with the mouse. Alternatively, someone can directly type references into formulas as C3:C7. References can be absolute, relative or mixed. Sometimes someone is required to specify an exact cell not only for the first formula that someone create but also for all others which will be modeled after it. eg. In the above case, someone want to find the sum of the marks obtained in English and Maths then someone include the cell addresses C3 and D3 in the addition. Someone can copy the formula to effect the addition of marks of all the five students. (How to do to this will be discussed later). Now, it is important to remember that Excel would adjust the reference to C3 and D3. The first formula would work, but the others won't since they refer to cells other than C3 and D3. To assure that formulas always refer to a specific cell it is better to make an absolute reference. Absolute addresses use the dollar sign ($) before both the row and column address. eg. to create an absolute reference to cell D4, someone should type D4. It is also possible to create mixed references that point to a specific column and a relative row eg. $A4 or a specific row and relative column eg.A$4.

It is also possible for someone to edit the reference someone have created. For this purpose, type directly in a formula. Alternatively execute the following steps:

- Select the cell containing the formula to be changed.

- In the Formula bar, select the reference to be changed.

- Press F4 repeatedly, all the while watching the reference change till someone get the desired effect.

8.4.6 Changing Reference Style :

Someone know that by default, Excel uses letters for column references and numbers for row references. It is however, possible for someone to change the referencing style. Someone can use numbers for both columns and rows as illustrated in the window below. When someone choose this option, the row references in the formulas must be preceded by the letter R and the column references must be preceded by the letter C.

Beginning with Excel / 201

The steps to change the reference style are :

- Choose Tools|Options.

- Click on the General tab to bring it in view.

- Choose R1C1 on the Reference Style area of the dialog box.

- Click OK. Excel will adjust all the formula references automatically.

8.4.7 Copying Entries and Equations :

When someone is creating large worksheets, it is very time consuming to type the same values over and over. But in Excel, it is possible to achieve this with ease. Also when someone create similar formulas in different cells, sometimes the only things that change in the formula are cell references. eg. As in our illustration we are adding the marks of student01 which are in columns C3 and D3 and storing the result in E3, we want a similar reference of C4, D4 and E4 for student02, C5, D5 and E5 for student05 and so on. All this can be achieved in Excel with the number of features available in the program.

AutoFill : AutoFill is one tool which allows someone to select cells of interest and make relative copies of them in adjacent cells. AutoFill can also be used to copy formulas. Highlight the cells of interest and then drag the fill outline using the square handle (called the fill handle) at the bottom corner of the active cell outline. The pointer changes into a large plus sign. As shown below, the student numbers have been filled using the AutoFill command. Someone can notice that Excel has automatically incremented the student number while executing AutoFill. If there are formulas, then Excel alters the cell references appropriately so the formulas use the appropriate values from the appropriate cells. This is possible because of relative referencing. Someone can see above, that Excel has automatically used the relative cell referencing and calculated the total as well as percentages for all marks entered. If however, someone do not want the

relative referencing to work, then someone should make use of absolute referencing in the

formulas.

Excel can also autofill days, months and years as well as time and

numbers.

8.5.1 Moving Cells:

In order to move cells, rows or columns someone have to first select them and then

use the drag and drop technique. The steps are:

- Highlight the cells someone want to move.

- Drag at their edges with the arrow shaped pointer.

- Release the mouse button to drop the selected item at the outlined position

- drag-and-drop warns someone if someone is overwriting non-blank cells. Click OK

to replace the previous cell contents.

8.5.2 Copying cells:

To copy cells, select them and copy with the Edit|Copy command and then

paste with the Edit|Paste command. Someone can also copy with Ctrl+C and paste

with Ctrl+V. It is also possible to copy with drag and drop. Go through the following

steps:

- Hold down the Ctrl key while dragging. The mouse pointer will have a small

plus sign next to it.

- When someone release the mouse, the selected cells will be copied to a

new location.

- Excel will ask someone to confirm the copy if it is going to cause over writing

in non blank cells. Click OK to confirm or Cancel to abort.

8.5.3 Sorting Cell data:

Groups of cells can be sorted in the ascending or descending order, using

upto three sort keys at once. The steps to be executed for sorting are:

- Select the rows and columns someone wish to sort. Someone can include headings

in the sorting if someone wish

- Choose Data|Sort

- Specify row or column sorting in the Sort Options dialog box. This box is reached by Data|Sort|Options.

- If someone wish to use headings as sort keys, pick that option in the dialog box.

- Pick the first sorting key. Also specify whether sorting is to be done in the ascending or descending order.

- If someone need to have additional sorts, move to the next key box and repeat the above process.

- This can be done upto three levels of sorting.

- Click OK.

Someone will now be able to view the sorted data.

8.5.4 Inserting Rows, Columns and Cells : Inserting Rows :

Select the entire row below the place where someone want a new blank row. Then choose Insert|Rows. A new blank row will be inserted. All the following rows will be pushed down and renumbered. If someone wish to insert multiple rows, select multiple rows before using the Insert command.

Inserting Columns:

To insert a column, point to the label of the column where someone want the new column to appear. Use the Insert|Column command. A new blank column will be inserted. All the columns that follow will be pushed to the right and renamed. To insert multiple columns, select multiple columns before using the Insert command.

Inserting Cells:

Highlight the area where someone wish to insert new blank cells and then use the command Insert|Cells. The Insert dialog box appears and asks someone whether someone want

to shift cells right or down or insert an entire row or column. Someone can enter the selection.

8.5.5 Deleting Parts of a worksheet:

To delete unwanted rows, columns or cells use the Edit|Delete command. This places them on the Clipboard. The space made by the deletion is also closed up. Remember that deletion of rows, columns or cells can affect formulas.

8.5.6 Clearing parts of a worksheet: Clearing removes the contents, but it does not

move the contents of the other cells to fill in the newly emptied space. Highlight the cells someone wish to clear and then press Del or use the Clear command from the Edit menu.

8.6 SUMMARY

Excel is one of the very advanced programs of Microsoft Office with the help of which someone can perform analysis of complex inter related columnar reports in workspaces called as **worksheet** or **spreadsheets.** Worksheets are made up of **cells** with array of rows and columns. Excel rows are generally identified with numbers and the columns are identified with letters. The address of each cell is its row and column label.

Someone can open the Excel program from the Start submenu or click on the Excel shortcut on the desktop (if it is present). The worksheet will open. Before entering or editing cell contents or before formatting or moving cells, they have to be selected. Someone can select cells with the help of keyboard or mouse. Remember someone can select a single cell or a group of cells. Ctrl+Shift+Spacebar will **select the entire worksheet.**

To extend selections in any direction someone can hold down the Shift key and press the appropriate arrow key.

To enter the text in the worksheet, someone should activate the cell where someone wish to insert the text. Someone can activate a cell by pointing to it and clicking it. As someone start typing, the text will appear in the active cell, as well as in the Formula bar. When someone press Enter, the text entry will be complete, and the text will be placed in the active cell. The Windows text editing features can be used to edit the text in the cells. In order to replace a text, simply activate a cell then type the new text and press Enter. The new text will replace the old text in the activated cell. Someone can make use of the buttons in the Formatting tool bar to make the text bold, change the Font, etc. The Format menu can also be used for additional choices of formatting. Someone can also create text boxes and place them anywhere someone want in the worksheet and type the text in the box. It is also possible to rotate text in text boxes.

Comments are used to hold notes which someone do not wish to display on the worksheets. These notes are attached to the cells and can be viewed on screen. Someone can also print comments.

The Edit menu contains the Undo and Repeat commands similar to those of Word. The Undo and Redo buttons are also available on the Standard toolbar. Numbers are often referred to as **values** in Excel. In addition to numbers someone can also enter the following symbols when typing numbers:

+ - ( ) , . $ % E e

Excel also accepts numbers in the scientific notation

Sometimes someone may want Excel to treat numbers, time entries or date like entries as text instead of numbers. In such a situation, precede the entry with a ' (single quotation mark). This mark is not displayed or printed, but the number entered after it would be treated as text entries.

Formulas are created when someone wish to add columns of numbers, divide one number by another, and such other computations. The formula should start with the = sign. Excel operators are divided into four general categories: arithmetic, comparison, text and reference. Arithmetic operators are the most commonly used.

In many situations when creating formulas, someone may be required to refer to a single cell only. A single cell reference refers to a specific cell. At other times someone may be required to refer to range of cells. Someone can specify references by clicking or dragging with the mouse. Alternatively, someone can directly type references into formulas. References can be absolute, relative or mixed.

Sometimes someone is required to specify an exact cell not only for the first formula that someone create but also for all others which will be modeled after it. To assure that formulas always refer to a specific cell it is better to make an absolute reference. Absolute addresses use the dollar sign ($) before both the row and column address. It is also possible for someone to edit the reference someone have created.

By default, Excel uses letters for column references and numbers for row references. It is however, possible for someone to change the referencing style. Someone can use numbers for both columns and rows.

AutoFill is one tool which allows someone to select cells of interest and make relative copies of them in adjacent cells. AutoFill can also be used to copy formulas. Highlight the cells of interest and then drag the fill outline using the square handle (called the fill handle) at the bottom corner of the active cell outline. The pointer changes into a large plus sign. If there are formulas, then Excel alters the cell references appropriately so the formulas use the appropriate values from the appropriate cells. This is possible because of relative referencing. Excel can also autofill days, months and years as well as time and numbers.

To move cells, rows or columns someone have to first select them and then use the drag and drop technique.

To copy cells, select them and copy with the Edit|Copy command and then paste with the Edit|Paste command. Someone can also copy with Ctrl+C and paste with Ctrl+V. It is also possible to copy with drag and drop.

Groups of cells can be sorted in the ascending or descending order, using upto three sort keys at once.

To insert a new row, select the entire row below the place where someone want a new blank row. Then choose Insert|Rows. A new blank row will be inserted. To insert a column point to the label of the column where someone want the new column to appear. Use the Insert|Column command. A new blank column will be inserted. To insert multiple columns, select multiple columns before using the Insert command.

To insert new blank cells highlight the area where someone wish to insert new blank cells and then use the command Insert|Cells.

To delete unwanted rows, columns or cells use the Edit|Delete command. Clearing removes the contents but it does not move the contents of the other cells to fill in the newly emptied space. Highlight the cells someone wish to clear and then press Del or use the Clear command from the Edit menu.

Chapter 9

9.1 INTRODUCTION

This chapter is devoted to the study of the formatting features in Excel. The formatting features in Excel can be used to enhance the appearance of the worksheets. Let us learn how to make use of the Standard toolbar ribbon, menus and the as well as keyboard shortcuts to change the appearance of cells in our worksheets. We shall study how to insert and remove manual page breaks, apply existing styles as well as create new styles, know how to use the Format Painter and many such features.

9.2 PAGE SETUP

Execute the following steps to make the Page setup as per the requirements of the project. This helps to see on the screen how the document will appear when printed.

- Choose Page Layout from menu. The Page Setup dialog box will appear.

- As per the requirement make changes to the page size, orientation, margins settings etc.

9.3 CHANGING COLUMN WIDTHS AND ROW HEIGHTS

In this section let us study the number of ways in which we can adjust the column widths and row heights in our Excel worksheets.

9.3.1 Automatically adjusting rows and columns:

Place the mouse pointer on or near the edge of a column label. The pointer will change into a thick black bar with arrows pointing left and right. Double click and the Best Fit feature of Excel will automatically make the left column wider or narrower as required to accommodate the longest entry in that particular column. If someone selects multiple columns before double clicking, then each selected column will switch to its best fit.

Row heights automatically increase to accommodate the tallest character in a row. Someone can also change single or multiple rows at the same time, with the same technique as that applied for columns. Point to a row(s) label. This will change the pointer to a thick horizontal bar with up and down pointing arrows. Double click and a best fit will automatically apply to the selected row/rows. Someone can also use the

AutoFit choices on the Row and Column submenus of the Format menu.

Remember if someone make changes to the cell contents later, then someone may be required to use the AutoFit again, since the column widths will not adjust automatically.

9.3.2 Dragging to change row and column sizes:

To make the own manual column width and row height changes, drag with

the pointers. Place the mouse pointer on or near the right edge of a row label. The

pointer changes into a thick black bar with arrows pointing left and right. When someone

drag, a light line will be displayed which shows the column width, which will result

when someone release the mouse button. Remember, if someone has selected multiple

columns then the dragging technique will make all of them of the same width. Try

using the same technique of dragging to change the row height and study the

results.

9.3.3 Using Submenu commands:

The Row| Height and Column| Width are the choices available in the **in the**

right click on column or row. These enable someone to specify row heights and

column widths. Column widths refer to the number of characters that will fit in the

cell, assuming that they are formatted in the Normal style. Row heights are

displayed and entered as points.

9.4 STYLES

Styles are a collection of formatting decisions. These include a number of format,

alignment instructions, border specifications etc. Styles are stored with the worksheets.

Someone can create new styles, edit existing styles and copy styles from other

worksheets also. Let us see how to do this in this section.

9.4.1 Applying Styles:

To apply an existing style go through the following steps :

- Select the cell or cells someone wish to format.

- Choose the Style option from the Format menu.

- Pick the desired style from the Style name list in the Style dialog box.

- Click on the name and click OK to apply the style.

The Normal style of Excel, displays and prints numbers using the General format which

is 10-point Sans-serif type, no borders and no shading. Remember someone can

redefine this style also

9.4.2 *Creating Styles:*

To create a style go through the following steps:

- Format the cell as per the liking.

- Keeping the cell active, choose Style from Excel's Format menu.

- Type a new style name in the Style Name portion of the Style dialog box. Click the Modify button to set these changes.

- Click OK to save the style. The new style will be added to the drop-down list and will be saved with the document.

9.4.3 Modifying Styles:

Go through the following steps to modify an existing style:

- Modify a cell which contains the style someone wish to change.

- Choose Format| Style and open the Style dialog box.

- Click the drop-down list button to display the drop-down list and choose the old style name from it. (Someone can also type the old-style name)

- Excel asks someone to confirm whether someone wish to modify the style based upon the changes which someone has made. Click Yes to redefine the style.

Remember when someone redefine a style, all the cells which have been formatted with that style will be redefined. With the Style dialog box, someone can see which style elements are used by the style eg. number formats, borders, patterns etc. Someone can also change these style elements by selecting the Modify button.

9.4.4 Format Codes:

Styles use format codes to determine how the numbers will appear. Someone can however, apply format codes directly to the selected cells without using styles. Someone can also alter existing format codes and create the own format codes.

Applying Format codes: A number of format codes are available in Excel, which are organized by type. These are available from the Format Cells dialog box. These codes can be used to format percentages, codes for currency etc. To apply a format code:

- Select the cell or cells to be reformatted

- Choose Format|Cells (Ctrl+1 shortcut can also be used)

- Bring the Number tab forward by clicking on it.

- Click on the category to display the available format.

- Double click on the format code someone wish to apply. Someone can also click on its name and then click the OK button.

- Someone may be required to reformat the columns if there are changes in the numbers' width.

Creating and Modifying format codes:

- If someone wish to apply format codes which are not offered by Excel, someone can execute the following steps:

- Select the cell or cells to be formatted.

- Choose the Format| Cells (Ctrl+1 shortcut).

- Bring the Number tab forward by clicking on Number tab.

- Click on Category to display the available format choices.

- Someone can now type the own text in the Type text box.

- After typing click OK. The new format code will be saved in the list. The selected cells will be formatted with this new code.

9.4.5 Format Painter:

This is a feature which allows someone to quickly copy a cell's format and spread it around elsewhere. The steps to use Format Painter are:

- Select the cell containing the desired format.

- Click on the Format Painter button. (It looks like a paintbrush).

- The mouse pointer changes into a cross and a paintbrush. Drag with it to select the cells which someone want to reformat.

- Release the mouse button. The cells will be reformatted. Adjust column widths if necessary.

9.4.6 Deleting Styles:

To delete unwanted styles, go through the following steps:

- Open the Style dialog box.

- If necessary, select the name of the style someone want to delete from the drop down Style Name list in the Style dialog box.

- Click the Delete button.

All cells formatted with the deleted style revert to the Normal style for the worksheet.

9.5 USING THE STANDARD AND FORMATTING TOOLBAR

Common formatting changes can be made from the Standard toolbar, from the Formatting toolbar and with the help of the keyboard. Someone should select the cells someone wish to format before using these buttons and keyboard short cuts.

9.5.1 A note about AutoFormat:

Excel has the AutoFormat feature which uses Table Formats. These are predefined collections of number formats, fonts, cell alignments, patterns, shading, column widths, row heights etc. which will auto format the cells someone specify. However, using the AutoFormat feature is not in the scope of this course material. We shall study manual formatting in the following sections.

9.5.2 Changing Font Sizes and Attributes :

Someone can use the Formatting toolbar to select the Font name and size. The Bold, Italic and Underline buttons can be used to add these effects to the data. For more advanced formatting options use the Font tab in the Format Cells dialog box.

9.5.3 Alignment :

Alignment buttons are available on the Standard and Formatting toolbars. The Alignment tab in the Format Cells dialog box also offers a number of choices like flushing the text left, right or center alignment. In this box also someone can specify how text and numbers will be positioned vertically within the selected cells. eg. The wrap option can be used to wrap words to fit the width of columns. Text can also be flipped with the orientation button.

9.5.4 Centering Text across columns :

In some situations, it may be necessary to float the contents of a particular cell across more than one column.

To do so:

- Activate the cell which is to be floated.

- Drag to select adjacent cells in the columns someone wish the text to float to.

- Click the Center Across Selection button on the Formatting toolbar. Someone can also

- Choose the Center Across Selection option in the Alignment tab of the Format

Cells dialog box. The text will center itself across the cells.

9.5.5 Changing Colors and Shading :

The Color button and the Text Color Button which are available on the Formatting

toolbar can be used to change the color of the selected text, cell shading etc. The

patterns tab in the Format Cells dialog box can also be used.

9.5.6 Border Buttons and Commands :

Borders can be used to set apart the related worksheet sections and to emphasize

totals and subtotals. Someone can also use them to enhance the appearance of the worksheet

or simply for decoration. Borders can be created by using the buttons available on the

Formatting toolbar by going through the following steps:

- Select the cell or cells for which someone wish to affect the border changes.

- To outline the selected text with borders on all sides, just click the Border button

arrow on the Formatting tool bar. The keyboard shortcut is Ctrl+Shift+&.

- Pick the desired border setting from the choices shown.

Someone can also construct custom borders in the Border tab of the Format Cells

dialog box. To do this the steps are:

- Select the cells.

- Open the Style dialog box and click Modify.

- Click the Border tab.

- Click to pick a border element (left, right etc.)

- Select the line type for the border from those available.

- Click OK to affect the selection.

9.6 PAGE BREAKS

Page break decisions are made automatically in Excel. In case someone wish to insert manual page breaks, choose Set Page Break option from the Insert menu. Dark dashed lines mark the new page breaks.

In order to remove page breaks activate the cell below and to the right of the break lines and choose the Remove Page Break command on the Insert menu.

9.7 HIDING ROWS AND COLUMNS

In Excel, it is possible to hide rows and columns without destroying their contents and then displaying them again whenever someone wish to see or edit them. Let us see how to do this.

To hide/unhide rows or columns using the Format menu:

- Select the row(s) or column(s) which someone want to hide.

- Choose the Hide and Unhide command (whichever applicable) on the Format menu's Row and Column choices.

To hide/unhide rows or columns with the help of a mouse: To hide rows and columns:

- Place the mouse pointer beneath the heading of the row(s) someone want to hide.

- Point beneath the appropriate number at the left edge of the worksheet.

- The pointer will change its shape to indicate that it is possible to change the row height.

- Drag upwards till the row(s) are so thin that they will disappear. The line which is between the visible and invisible rows becomes darker than the rest. The row numbers are also not consecutive.

Follow the same method to hide columns, and drag to the right on column letters.

To unhide rows and columns: Slowly move the pointer over the dark lines in row or column labels. At some position, the dark bar between two arrow heads will split indicating that someone can drag the rows or columns back to a useful size. Someone can also

select the columns or rows to either side of the hidden column or row and then use the Unhide button in the Column Width and Row Height dialog boxes.

9.8 USING NAMES

In Excel someone can name a range of cells, name formulas and so on. The name appears in the Name box which is on the left side of the Formula bar. Named items are easy to find with the Edit|Go To command or by using F5. Someone can define names themselves or alternatively, Excel also creates names for someone by using the labels in the worksheets. Names can be up to 255 characters long with the first character being an alphabet.

9.8.1 Creating Names:

Excel can create names of selected cells based on the row and column headings. For this purpose:

- Select the cells someone wish to name, along with their headings. -Choose Name from the Insert menu.

- Choose Create from the submenu. The Create Names dialog box appears.

- Now choose the label locations which someone wish to use as names. Excel will use these labels to assign names automatically, modifying them if necessary.

9.8.2 Defining names by them selves

If someone wish to give names to selected cells manually, go through the following steps:

- Select the cells someone want to name.

- Choose the Name option from the Insert menu.

- Choose Define from the submenu.

- The Define Name dialog box appears.

- Excel will propose a name if it can. Someone can click OK to accept this proposed name or type a name. Then click Add.

9.8.3 Seeing Named item:

To see what is included in a named item or range, pick a name from the Name Box's drop-down list. Excel will select the named item or range in the worksheet.

9.9 SPLITTING WINDOWS

Excel documents windows can be split into two or four separately scrollable panes that make it easy to see different parts of the worksheet at the same time. Let us see how to do this. There are two ways in which this can be achieved.

Using the Split Command:

Use the Split command on the View menu to create four panes in the neighborhood of the active cell. Someone can see that each pane will have its own scroll tools. To remove the split someone can use the Remove Split command. This command appears on Excel's Window menu whenever a window is split.

Splitting Windows with the help of a mouse :

Let us see how the panes can be split with the help of a mouse. In a single pane worksheet, there are thick black lines just above the top of the vertical scroll arrow and

Formatting Features of Excel / 219

to the right of the right horizontal scroll arrow. These are called as split boxes. Someone can drag on either one or both in order to create panes. Double clicking on a split pane will remove its panes.

9.10 SUMMARY

The formatting features in Excel can be used to enhance the appearance of the worksheets. The Page Setup can be used to make changes to the page size, orientation, margins settings etc.

The column widths and row heights in Excel worksheets can be adjusted automatically, where row heights automatically increase to accommodate the tallest character in a row. Someone can also change single or multiple rows at the same time. Someone can also use the **AutoFit** choices on the Row and Column submenus of the Format menu. To make the own manual column width and row height changes, drag with the pointers. The Row| Height and Column| Width are the choices available in the **in the right click on** particular column or row. These enable someone to specify row heights and column widths. Column widths refer to the number of characters that will fit in the cell, assuming that they are formatted in the Normal style. Row heights are displayed and entered as points.

Styles are a collection of formatting decisions. These include a number of format, alignment instructions, border specifications etc. Styles are stored with the worksheets themselves. Someone can create new styles, edit existing styles and copy styles from other worksheets also. The Normal style of Excel, displays and prints numbers using the General format which is 10-point Sans-serif type, no borders and no shading. When someone redefine a style, all the cells which have been formatted with that style will be redefined. With the Style dialog box, someone can see which style elements are used by the style. Styles use format codes to determine how the numbers will appear. Someone can however, apply format codes directly to the selected cells without using styles. Someone can also alter existing format codes and create the own format codes. **Format Painter** is a feature which allows someone to quickly copy a cell's format and spread it around elsewhere.

Common formatting changes can be made from the Standard toolbar, from the Formatting toolbar and with the help of the keyboard. Someone should select the cells someone wish to format before using these buttons and keyboard short cuts.

Excel has the AutoFormat feature which uses Table Formats. These are predefined collections of number formats, fonts, cell alignments, patterns, shading, column widths, row heights etc. which will autoformat the cells someone specify.

Someone can use the Formatting toolbar to select the Font name and size. For more advanced formatting options use the Font tab in the Format Cells dialog box. Alignment buttons are available on the Standard and Formatting toolbars. The Alignment tab in the Format Cells dialog box also offers a number of choices like flushing the text left, right or center alignment. The wrap option can be used to wrap words to fit the width of columns. Text can also be flipped with the orientation button. The Color button and the Text Color Button which are available on the Formatting toolbar can be used to change the color of the selected text, cell shading etc. The patterns tab in the Format Cells dialog box can also be used.

Borders can be used to set apart the related worksheet sections and to emphasize totals and subtotals. Someone can also use them to enhance the appearance of the worksheet or simply for decoration. Borders can be created by using the buttons available on the Formatting toolbar. Someone can also construct custom borders in the Border tab of the Format Cells dialog box.

Page break decisions are made automatically in Excel. In case someone wish to insert manual page breaks, choose Set Page Break option from the Insert menu. Dark dashed lines mark the new page breaks. In order to remove page breaks, activate the cell below and to the right of the break lines and choose the Remove Page Break command on the Insert menu. In Excel, it is possible to hide rows and columns without destroying their contents and then displaying them again whenever someone wish to see or edit them. Someone can hide/ unhide rows and columns using the Format menu, or with the help of a mouse.

In Excel someone can name a range of cells, name formulas and so on. The name appears in the Name box which is on the left side of the Formula bar. Named items are easy to find with the Edit|Go To command or by using F5. Someone can define names them self or alternatively Excel also creates names for someone by using the labels in the worksheets. Names can be upto 255 characters long with the first character being an alphabet.

In order to see what is included in a named item or range, pick a name from the Name Box's drop-down list. Excel will select the name item or range in the worksheet.

Excel documents windows can be split into two or four separately scrollable panes that make it easy to see different parts of the worksheet at the same time. There are two ways in which this can be achieved: Usi ng the Split Command and Splitting Windows with the help of a mouse.

Chapter 10

10.1 INTRODUCTION

This chapter is devoted to the introduction of functions, charts and graphics in Excel. Remember that a detailed study of each of these topics is not included in this study material. These are advanced features of Excel, which the student should study and master with continuous usage. A separate section each for functions, charts and graphs is given, to provide a general idea of how to use these features of Excel. Study them and use them to improve the expertise of using Excel.

10.2 FUNCTIONS IN EXCEL

10.2.1 Introduction:

Functions are powerful tools that help to perform complex computations. The functions in Excel facilitate engineering computations, text manipulations etc. There are two types of functions in Excel viz. worksheet functions and macro functions. We shall attempt to gain an introduction to worksheet functions only. Worksheet functions can be used by themselves as stand alone formulas, or they can be built into more complex formulas which someone create.

10.2.2 Parts of a function:

Functions consist of a function name and arguments. eg. SQRT(number); here SQRT is the function name and number is the positive argument whose square root would be computed with this function. It may so happen that some functions do not need arguments. Some functions may have arguments which are required along with optional arguments which may not be absolutely necessary to execute that function. Multiple arguments should be separated by commas. Functions can also take other functions as arguments eg. = ROUND(SQRT(A2), 2). This would compute the square root of the contents of A2 and then round the answer to two decimal places.

Worksheet functions have been divided into nine categories viz. Database, Date and Time, Financial, Information, Logical, Lookup and Reference, Mathematical and Trigonometric, Statistical and Text.

10.2.3 The Function Wizard:

The Function Wizard greatly simplifies the use of the functions. To use the Function Wizard:

- Activate the cell where someone want to paste the function.

- Begin the formula with the equal to (=) sign and place the insertion point where someone want to insert the function.

- Click the insert function button on the formula Menu bar. The Wizard's first step window appears as shown below:

The functions as per the categories mentioned above are listed by the Wizard. In addition, it also shows the Most Recently Used and All options.

☐ Pick the category of the interest from this list. The list of functions for that particular category is listed at the right. Scroll through the list to select the desired function.

Introduction to Functions, Charts and Graphics / 225

☐ The function name is displayed in the Name box on the Formula bar and its name and arguments re shown near the bottom left corner of the Paste Function dialog box.

☐ Click OK. The second dialog box of the Wizard appears.

☐ Someone can now type directly in the entry boxes provided in this window. Alternatively, someone can also make use of the mouse to point to cells containing the data which someone want to use as arguments.

☐ As someone are working, the Wizard shows the results of the calculation in the Value area at the top right corner of the dialog box.

☐ Click OK once someone has completed the formula. The Wizard now pastes the function into the active cell and displays the results of the current arguments in the cell. Someone can see the equation in the Formula bar.

10.2.4 Commonly used functions:

Let us see some of the commonly used functions in Excel by category.

1. **Date and Time Functions:** Some date and time functions are

available which return the current date and/or time. Other functions do math in addition to just returning just date and time. eg. = NOW() is a function which will display the current date, followed by the current time, in the selected cell and then update the contents of the cell every time the worksheet is recalculated. Different date and time types are found in the Number tab of the Format Cells dialog box. There is a number of ways in which Excel can display date and time.

2. **Engineering Functions:** These functions are available but they require the

Analysis Toolbar add in macro to be installed on the system.

3. **Financial Functions:** An example of a financial function is PMT(). The syntax of the function is PMT(rate, nper, pv, fv, type) where rate is the interest rate per period, nper indicates the total number of payments, pv is the present value i.e the total amount that the series of payments is worth now, fv is the future value and type is either 0 or 1. Both these arguments are optional. If time is entered as 0 or omitted then it indicates that payments will be made at the end of each period. Entering a value 1 for type indicates that payments will be made at the beginning of the period.

4. **Information Functions:** An example of this type of function is ISNONTEXT(). This function will tell the formula whether a cell entry is not text. Such types of functions inspect the data and return information.

5. **Logical Functions:** IF() is an example of logical function in Excel.

6. **Lookup and Reference functions:** They can be used to create invoices that can look up and insert different unit prices based on the quantities purchased. These functions can inspect rows, columns or arrays.

7. **Math and Trig:Function :** SQRT () and SUM() are mathematical functions. Math and Trig functions can refer to cell references, names or plain numbers. RAND() is a function which produces evenly

distributed random numbers greater than or equal to 0 and less than 1, each time Functions someone recalculate.

8. **Statistical Functions:** A number of statistical functions are provided, eg. AVDEV().

9. **Text Functions:** These functions are useful to manipulate or analyze strings of text in cells, eg. CLEAN () is a function which removes all non printable characters in a cell. UPPER () is a function which will convert text to uppercase.

These functions were just provided as an introduction to the student. There is a lot more to be studied in this area. This can be pursued by the student.

10.3 CHARTS IN EXCEL

Excel helps someone to create charts in two or three dimensions on the basis of the data in the worksheet. Before actually starting to create charts let us first familiarize ourselves with some term related to charts in Excel.

10.3.1 Chart Terminology:

1. **Chart Data Series:** A chart data series is a collection of related values that are plotted on the chart.

Introduction to Functions, Charts and Graphics / 227

2. **Data Markers:** Data markers are the bars, pie wedges, dots, pictures etc. which are used to represent a particular data point i.e. a single value in a series. When charts have more than one data series the markers for each series usually took different.

3. **Axes:** An axis is a reference line denoting one of the dimensions of a chart. Excel can plot up to three axes X, Y and Z. Normally the X-axis runs horizontally from left to right, the Y-axis runs vertically from bottom to top.

4. **Category Names:** These correspond to the worksheet labels for the data which is being plotted along the X axis.

4. **Chart Data Series Names:** These usually correspond to worksheet

labels for the data being plotted on the Y-axis. Data series names are usually displayed in a box (called a legend) alongside a sample of the color, shade, or pattern used for each data series.

6. **Tick Marks and Gridlines:** Short lines which intersect an axis to separate parts of a series scale or category are called tick marks. **Grid lines** are optional. Someone can add gridlines using the Format|Select Grid Lines option.

7. **Chart Text**: : The Chart Wizard automatically adds text for things like charts and data labels. Someone can add the own text too.

8.

10.3.2 Creating Charts with the Chart Wizard :

Let us now see how to use the Chart Wizard. There is a simple step process and each step is explained herewith along with the windows that appear for each step.

Start by creating a worksheet containing the data someone wish to chart. Let us use our sample document which we have already created for the students and the marks obtained by them as an illustration. Next, select the data someone want to be included in the chart. Do not include any empty rows or columns. Click on the Chart In insert menu. Then select the chart type as visible in following figure.

The chart will be on the same sheet where someone selected the data. Now by right clicking on that chart someone will get select data option which is used to select another range etc.

If someone want to change the Titles of Y, X-axis then click on the edit button on the right pane of **Select data sources** figure. Someone can also change the chart type by using following step: -

Right click on chart->select change chart type

10.3.3 Resizing and Moving charts:

Charts can be easily resized by dragging the little handles which surround the selected chart. When someone click in the chart it will be selected and handles will appear.

10.3.4 Adding Charts Notes and Arrows:

Many times someone may need to explain certain item on the chart. To do this someone can add notes and arrows in the chart.

☐ **Adding Notes :** For this purpose go through the following steps :

- Click on the Text button. (In the Drawing toolbar)

- Drag to create the outline of the text box of the desired size and shape.

- Now someone can type and edit the text.

- Someone can also resize or move the box by pointing to it and clicking on any edge. Once someone select it, someone will get the familiar eight handles which someone can use for moving or resizing. Also remember someone can format the text to the liking with the text related menu commands.

☐ **Drawing and Formatting arrows :** To draw an arrow in the chart:

- Click on the Drawing button of the Standard toolbar.

- Click the Arrow button on the toolbar.

- The pointer will change into cross hairs. Point to the position where someone want the arrow to start and then drag to the ending point.

- When someone release the mouse button, the arrow will appear.

Remember someone can reposition and/or change the length of the arrow. Someone can also define arrow styles, colors, thickness etc. with the help of the Format Object dialog box. To do this, someone must double click on the arrow.

10.3.5 Editing charts:

Let us see some of the editing options for charts in this section.

Changing the chart type and its formats: After someone have created a chart, someone can change its type at any later time. Click on the chart type list of the Chart toolbar. A palette of chart choices will appear. Select a new chart type of the liking.

Changing the Data Series Ranges: To change the data series ranges select a chart and click on the Chart Wizard button. Now in the window that appears (the first window which appears when someone create the chart with the Chart Wizard) someone can specify the new data range. Someone can go further to Step 2, to change the appearance of the chart.

Selecting and Editing chart components: It is possible for someone to edit only specific parts of a chart like text, gridlines, shading used for markers etc. by either single clicking or double clicking on them. To change the appearance of the chart title, double click on it. The Format Object dialog box will open and someone can modify the appearance of the title. To edit the title contents, click to select the object and then select the text by clicking on it. If someone want to select a data series, click on any marker in the series. Someone will then see a description of the data series in the Formula bar. Here someone can edit the series definition if someone so desire. Someone can also select a single data marker by holding down the CTRL key while pointing. To select a gridline, click exactly on the gridline. Someone can also select just the plot area by clicking in any part of the plot area which is not occupied by things like gridlines or markers. To select an axis, simply click on it. To select an entire chart, click anywhere outside of the plot area, but not on item like titles or legends.

Changing Worksheet Values by Dragging Chart Parts: Create a worksheet and the corresponding chart. Click once on the data marker someone wish to resize. Click again. The data marker someone clicked upon will be selected. It will have some small black selection markers. When someone drag on the top center black marker, someone will be able to move that selected part of the chart and automatically change the numbers in the corresponding worksheet cells.

10.3.6 Printing Charts :

By default, Excel will print all the charts. If someone wish to display but not print an embedded chart, then select the chart, remove the check mark from the Print Object option which is available in the Properties tab of the Format Object dialog box.

If a chart is a separate worksheet, it can be printed like any other Excel worksheet. Someone can use the Page Setup and Print preview options before printing. Someone can add headers, footers etc.

10.3.7 Deleting Charts : The simplest way to delete a chart is to select it and the press the Del key. Separate chart worksheets can be deleted in the same way as someone would delete any Windows worksheet.

10.3.8 To Set the Default Chart type : By default the Chart Wizard command normally creates new charts using the Column chart type and format 1. This is also known as the **preferred chart style.** Someone can also define a different preferred style. For this purpose, go through the following steps :

- Select a chart from the current worksheet which someone would like

to be the default chart type.

- Right click on that chart.

- Select Chart Type.

- Choose the set Default Chart Type from the bottom button.

10.3.9 Overlaying charts: Sometimes someone will want to overlay one kind of chart on another. One easy method to do this is to choose the **Combination chart type.** It creates two layers on the chart. It displays half of the layers as bars and the other half as lines.

10.4 GRAPHICS IN EXCEL

Worksheets in Excel can include imported graphic images, item which someone drew themselves, text boxes, arrows etc. Graphics are mainly used to enhance the appearance of the documents and also as an integral part of a presentation.

10.4.1 Creating and Placing Graphic objects :

Graphics can be placed anywhere in the worksheets. They can also be moved, resized and restyled. Someone can import graphics from WordArt, ClipArt gallery etc. by using the insert command. Someone can also paste parts of the

Excel worksheet into other types of documents. This means someone can export

Excel Graphics.

Once someone have inserted graphics in the worksheet the steps to resize it are :

- Select the graphic by pointing to it with the mouse.

- The handle appears which someone can use to drag and resize the graphic.

- If someone wish to change both the dimensions at the same time, drag the corner handles.

10.4.2 Positioning Graphics in the Worksheet:

To move an object, simply select it and drag it with the mouse. To move multiple item, SHIFT- click on each of them. Someone can then drag them all at once with the mouse and release when someone have placed them at the desired position. Someone can also select graphics, copy or cut them to the Clipboard and paste them elsewhere.

10.5 SUMMARY

Functions are powerful tools that help to perform complex computations. The functions in Excel facilitate engineering computations, text manipulations etc. There are two types of functions in Excel viz. worksheet functions and macro functions. Functions consist of a function name and arguments. It may so happen that some functions do not need arguments. Some functions may have arguments which are required along with optional arguments which may not be absolutely necessary to execute that function. Multiple arguments should be separated by commas. Functions can also take other functions as arguments. Worksheet functions have been divided into nine categories viz. Database, Date and Time, Financial, Information, Logical, Lookup and Reference, Mathematical and Trigonometric, Statistical and Text. The Function Wizard greatly simplifies the use of the functions.

Charts: Excel helps someone to create charts in two or three dimensions on the basis of the data in the worksheet. A chart **data series** is a collection of related values that are plotted on the chart. **Data markers** are the bars, pie wedges, dots, pictures etc. which are used to represent a particular data point i.e. a single value in a series. When charts have more than one data series, the markers for each series usually look different. An **axis** is a reference line denoting one of the dimensions of a chart. Excel can plot up to three axes X, Y and Z. Normally the X-axis runs horizontally from left to right, the Y-axis runs vertically from bottom to top.

Category Names correspond to the worksheet labels for the data which is being plotted along the X axis. **Chart Data Series Names** correspond to worksheet labels for the data being plotted on the Y-axis. Data series names are usually displayed in a box (called a legend) alongside a sample of the color, shade, or pattern used for each data series. Short lines which intersect an axis to separate parts of a series scale or category are called **tick marks.** Grid lines are optional. Someone can add gridlines using the Format|Select Grid Lines option. The Chart Wizard automatically adds text for things like charts and data labels. Someone can add the own text too.

Creating Charts with the Chart Wizard has some different step process. The first window of the chart wizard appears and displays the various chart types which are available and many formats for each of those types. The various chart types included are column, bar, line, pie, doughnut, radar etc. The second window shows someone the range of the data to be charted i.e the source data and someone can alter the range if someone so desire. The third window shows the formatting options which will be different for each chart type. Someone can add chart titles for the chart itself as well as for its axes. The titles will appear in the Sample Chart area as someone type them. The final window of the wizard asks where someone wish to place the chart. Excel charts can be either an integral part of the current worksheet or they can be separate chart worksheets in a workbook which are linked to selected worksheet data. Normally the Chart Wizard will create charts in the current worksheet only. If someone wish to create a separate chart worksheet selects the As a new sheet option.

Charts can be easily resized by dragging the little handles which surround the selected chart. Many times, someone may need to explain certain item on the chart. To do this someone can add notes and arrows in the chart. After someone have created a chart, someone can change its type at any later time. To change the data series ranges select a chart and click on the Chart Wizard button. Now in the window that appears (the first window which appears when someone create the chart with the Chart Wizard) someone can specify the new data range. It is possible for someone to edit only specific parts of a chart like text, gridlines, shading used for markers etc. by either single clicking or double clicking on them.

By default, Excel will print all the charts. If someone wish to display but not print an embedded chart, then select the chart, remove the check mark from the Print Object option which is available in the Properties tab of the Format Object dialog box. The simplest way to delete a chart is to select it and the press the Del key. Someone can use the Clear command on the Edit menu also. Separate chart worksheets can be deleted in the same way as someone would delete any Windows worksheet.

By default, the Chart Wizard command normally creates new charts using the

Column chart type and format 1. This is also known as the **preferred chart style.** Someone can also define a different preferred style. Sometimes someone will want to overlay one kind of chart on another. One easy method to do this is to choose the **Combination chart type.** It creates two layers on the chart. It displays half of the layers as bars and the other half as lines. Trendlines are used to plot the direction of data in a series, it is easy to add trendlines to Excel bar, column, area and scatter chart types. Worksheets in Excel can include imported graphic images, item which someone drew, text boxes, arrows etc. Graphics are mainly used to enhance the appearance of the documents and also as an integral part of a presentation. Graphics can be placed anywhere in the worksheets. They can also, be moved, resized and restyled. Someone can import graphics from WordArt ClipArt gallery etc. by using the Insert|Object command. Someone can also paste parts of the Excel worksheet into other types of documents. This means someone can export Excel Graphics.

CHAPTER 11

PowerPoint Basics

11.1 INTRODUCTION

With PowerPoint someone can create, update and sort slide based professional looking presentation materials. PowerPoint is a program which helps someone to create:

- black and white or color overhead transparencies

- 35mm slides

- computer screen and video slide shows with special effects

- presentation files and printed meeting handouts

- detailed speaker notes

- printed and onscreen presentation outlines.

Remember that PowerPoint too, has many features and techniques that someone has been using with Word and Excel. When someone has made a presentation in PowerPoint, it is easy for someone to practice the presentation at the desk before the actual presentation.

11.2 POWERPOINT TERMINOLOGIES

Let us now familiarize ourselves with some common term used in PowerPoint before actually beginning to create slides :

Slides : Someone can create and edit individual pages in PowerPoint. These are called slides.

Speaker's Notes: Speaker's notes are usually printed on paper and they can be the exact text of the speech, reminder notes, backup information etc.

Handouts: Handouts are paper copies of all or some of the slides to be given to the audience. They can be one per page or be reduced so that three to six fit on a sheet of paper.

Presentation Files: All the PowerPoint slides for a particular project are kept in a single PowerPoint file Called a **presentation.** The presentation file normally has a extension .PPTX. A presentation file can have one or many slides. If someone have recorded sounds or added speaker's notes then these elements will also be stored in the presentation file

Masters: Master slides hold information that will appear on multiple slides in the presentation. e.g. If someone want to put the company name, logo etc. on each slide then someone can add it to the master for that presentation.

It is also possible to create separate masters for handouts and speaker's notes within each presentation. PowerPoint itself has a variety of preprogrammed masters which someone can use. Someone can use them as they are, modify them or create the own masters.

Color Schemes: In PowerPoint, someone can define the own rules for applying colors or shades of gray to the various components of the presentation. Someone can specify the background colors for a slide. The colors for the headings etc.

Templates: A PowerPoint template consists of a master and color scheme. In PowerPoint there are 160 predefined templates. To change the look of a presentation, someone can just apply a different template to an existing presentation. This will completely change the appearance of the template.

Ribbons: Ribbons are located at the top of the page where Taskbar used to be in earlier version. The ribbon displays all useful new commands and tools.

The table shown below will help someone to learn the different ribbons and its uses.

Ribbons Uses

Home Editing options, Change the font, paragraph and heading style

Insert Inserts Header, footer, Symbols, tables, links Design Changes colors, font and effects, Background style & graphics Animation Sets custom animation and slide transition Slide show Views presentation, Rehearse timing and settings for slide show

Review Protects document and View Changes Window Lay outs

11.3 VIEWS

Before beginning to create presentations, it is important to study the various views offered by PowerPoint for entering, editing and previewing information. Someone can select these views from the Standard toolbar. These views include:

- Slide view
- Slide Sorter view
- Notes Page view
- Slide Show view

Someone can also switch views by using the View menu or the view buttons at the bottom left of the PowerPoint window.

Let us now obtain a brief information about these views.

Outline view: While in the outline view, someone can easily rearrange individual item. Someone

can also collapse item in this view which can enable someone to see just the headings or just the names of each slide.

Slide View: The slide view shows how the finished slides will look. Someone can see the background colors, shades etc. Someone can edit text and other slide elements while in the Slide view. Use the PgUp and PgDn keys or the scroll bar to move from slide to slide.

Slide Sorter View: This view lets someone see the thumbnails i.e reduced size slide images. While in this view, someone can drag slides and move them. Someone can also specify the types of

slide transitions in this view.

Notes Page View: This view is used to create and see notes. It shows a miniature slide image and provides the text area for presenter's notes.

To enter a note :

Click in the text area beneath the slide. The box outline will change appearance. Type and edit in the note box.

Slide Show View: The Slide Show View can be used to rehearse the presentation as well as for actual video presentation of the slide shows. To leave the Slide Show View someone have to press Esc or choose End Show option from the pop up menu.

11.4 CREATING PRESENTATIONS

We can start the PowerPoint program in many ways eg. someone can use **New** option from the office Button. The A New presentation window will appear with Blank presentation option.

11.4.1 Design Themes:

It is possible for someone to manually change the background, type styles and other design elements on the slides. However, if someone wish to change the appearance of all the slides the best way is to change the appearance of master slides. This will change the design elements for all the slides in the presentation. Someone can do this using the design Ribbon.

- Start with New presentation
- Click on Design menu bar to open design ribbon Design
- Choose appropriate theme .
- A number of design templates are available from which someone can select a template of the choice. Click on a template and someone will be able to see a thumbnail of the resulting look in the preview area. It will give someone a general idea of how the presentation will look with the selected template.
- Once someone has selected the template of the choice click Apply.
- PowerPoint will switch back to the presentation and within a moment someone will be able to see one of the slides with the features of the applied template.

11.4.2 Masters:

Masters make it easy for someone to specify common design elements that someone wish to include throughout the presentation. Masters can contain elements like logos, backgrounds, color schemes, date and time stampings etc. Each presentation has a master for:

- Slides
- Outlines
- Handouts
- Speaker's notes

There are a variety of predefined masters available in PowerPoint. They are stored in templates. Someone can pick the master of the choice for each presentation. Someone can even change to different masters after someone have created the presentations. A typical slide master is as shown below. It contains common elements for all slides or projects.

Remember that whatever changes someone make to the master will affect all the slides in the current presentation. Someone can however overrule master setting for individual slides or printout pages. A master will typically include: Title text, Body text, Color schemes, Background shading, Presentation title, Date Stamp, Time Stamp as shown in the above slide.

11.4.3 Exiting Masters: To change data in a master:

- Open the presentation

- Select View|Master|Slide

- Make the necessary changes to the slide as per the requirement. Remember someone can also move item on the master as well as resize them. To

move an item, click on it to select it and then drag it with the mouse pointer. To resize the master element, select it and then drag the black handles (which appear after selecting it) to change the size and shape.

- View all the slides to see the effect of the changes.

11.4.4 Adding Slides:

Someone can add i.e. insert new slides while in the Outline, Slide or Slide Sorter views.

The new slides can be created by inserting an Auto Lay out. Someone can also insert slides from other presentations. Someone can also insert elements from other program like Word, Excel etc. In this section let us see how to insert slides manually:

New slides are always inserted after the current slide. The steps are:

- Switch to the Slide, Slide Sorter or Outline view.

- Click to select the slide just before the point where someone want the new slide.

- Choose Home | New Slide option.

If someone are in Outline view, a new slide will be inserted which uses the same

Lay out as the preceding style. In the Slide view or the Slide Sorter view, someone will be presented with the New Slide Auto Lay out dialog box. Select an Auto Lay out and click OK.

The new slide will be inserted and the slides following it will be renumbered.

11.4.4 Changing the Lay out:

A number of slide Lay outs for common slide making tasks are provided by

Microsoft. There are a number of things which are common to most presentations like the title slide, bulleted lists, charts etc.

To change the lay out slides

- Open the presentation.

- click the home menu to display the ribbon

- select the Lay out button f rom sl ide sect ion

- Select from the Auto Lay out choices the one someone want and click OK.

- Save the presentation after someone have finished working with the new slide.

11.4.5 Deleting Slides :

To delete an unwanted slide, select it in any view and choose Home | Delete slide
option.

11.5.1 Editing and Moving text:

In PowerPoint text is kept in title objects and body objects. These objects are
rectangular areas which are surrounded by nonprinting lines. To work with the text in an
object, first select the object and then the text within that object. Someone can work in Slide
view, Outline view or Note Pages view.

Inserting text : Point and click within an object. Move the insertion point to the place in
the text where someone wish to insert new text and begin typing. Remember to keep text in a
particular slide limited. Someone can increase number of slides if required. If someone insert
too
much of text in a slide it may be too smaller making it difficult for the audience to read.

Inserting Bullet Item : Place the insertion point where someone want the new item and
press Enter. PowerPoint will automatically add a new line preceded by a bullet. If the
bulleted line insertion contains a large amount of text someone may have to create additional
slides or format the bulleted item appropriately. This is because PowerPoint won't add
new pages to fit the item automatically if they tend to fall outside the body object.

Deleting Text : Select unwanted text and press Del.

Moving Text : If someone have to reorganize multiple item it is best to work in the Outline
view. But for minor alternations within the same object someone can work in the Slide view.
Just
select the text and then drag and drop as someone do in Microsoft Word. If someone have to
move

text to other objects, to other slides or to other presentations :

- Select the text to be moved

- Cut it

- Switch to the destination slide (if someone want to place in a different slide).

- Select the title or body object where someone want to place the text.

- Click to position the insertion point where someone want to place the text and use Paste.

11.5.2 Working in Outline View :

The Outline view is the best preferred view when someone wish to make major changes to the content of the text. Outline view allows someone to see the entire text or just the selected heading levels. Someone can change the order of slides by dragging them from place to place. Someone can also move text around on its slide or move text from one slide to another.

Someone can increase and decrease the amount of information which is displayed in the Outline view. Click on the buttons on the left edge of the Outline view screen. To reveal all the text, click on the Show All button. This will bring all the text back into view.

To expand or collapse the details for selected slides (or portions of the slides) go through the following steps :

- Select the slide or slides or the portions of slides as may be necessary.

- To expand i.e. reveal information in the selected area, use the Expand Selection button (+ sign).

- PowerPoint will expand the selected area and someone can see the additional details.

- To collapse i.e. hide details, use the Collapse Selection option. (- sign)

Headings : In PowerPoint titles and headings can have different levels. Thus it becomes very easy to create multilevel indented lists. At the top level is the slide title itself. Remember different levels can have their own different appearances like font size, colors etc.

To move from one level to another:

- Select an item which someone wish to promote or demote.

- Point at the left edge of the item. The mouse pointer changes to a four headed arrow.

- Drag left to promote and drag right to demote the selected item.

- A vertical line will appear to show someone the pending new level of the item being-dragged.

- Release the mouse button. The item will take its new indent level and appearance.

11.5.3 Find and Replace text:

The Edit & Find command allows searching for text and with the Edit &

Replace command someone can search for as well as change text.

To Replace Text : To replace all occurrences of a particular text:

- Save the presentation.

- Click the Office Button on the ribbon

- Enter the text which someone want to replace in the Find What box.

- Enter the text with which someone want to replace the text in the Replace With box.

- Choose the Match Case option to have exact replacement with case matching.

- Click Find Next. PowerPoint searches for a match.

- Click Replace to replace the first match found and then click Find Next to

continue. Someone can select the Replace All option to replace all occurrences.

Finding Text : In the Find dialog box in PowerPoint, there is also a Replace

button in case if someone desire to replace the found text with the new text.

- Choose the Editing |Find option from Home menu

- Specify the text someone want to find. Someone can also specify whether someone wish to

match case or not.

- Use the Find Next button to find the matches or Close to quit the search.

- Make use of the Replace button to replace text if someone so desire.

11.5.4 Text Formatting :

PowerPoint automatically chooses fonts, colors, character sizes etc. Someone can

however manually override these. Some of these options are examined in this section.

Someone can use the formatting toolbar buttons, the keyboard shortcuts, the Font

command options to change the font, font size etc.

Underline Text : To underline text, select the text and use the Formatting toolbar's

Underline button or Ctrl+U shortcut.

Font Colors : Use the Text Color button or right click on Text then select Font option and the color list will appear in the dialog box. Someone can select the color of the choice.

Changing Case : Someone can use the Font| All caps command to change case of the selected text. When someone select this option, the dialog box appears which shows someone a list

of available choices.

Line and Paragraph Spacing : It is possible to change the amount of space between lines, space before and after paragraphs, in body objects and in title objects.

- Select the line(s) or the text object(s) someone want to reformat

- Press right click button of mouse

- The Line Spacing dialog box will appear. Here someone can specify new settings in either number of lines or points.

- Click OK to make changes.

Copying Text Styles : There are two ways in which someone can copy text formatting : First is, use the Pick Up and Apply command which is available in the Format menu and in the other use a toolbar button.

By using the **Pick Up and Apply** command :

- Select the text containing the formatting someone wish to copy.

- Choose Pick Up Style from the Format menu.

- Select the text which someone want to reformat.

- Choose Apply Text Style from the Format menu. The selected text will now be reformatted.

By using the **Format Painter** toolbar button :

- Select the text containing the formatting someone wish to copy.

- Click on the Format Painting toolbar button. The mouse pointer changes shape.

- Select the text which someone want to reformat.

- The selected text will now be reformatted.

Selecting Bullets for Lists :

It is possible for someone to use almost any character from any font as a bullet in the bulleted lists. Someone can alter the size and color of bullets as well.

- Select the bulleted item someone wish to modify.

- Choose Home Button from paragraph group select Bullets option.

This will open the Bullets dialog box.

- Choose the Font of the choice. Someone can click on individual symbols to see their enlarged view.

- Change the color if someone so desire.

- Preview the work, by clicking on the Preview button.

Someone can also set the size using the Size text box. Remember size of bullets is specified as a percentage of the text size.

Someone click OK to save changes, cancel otherwise.

Aligning Text:

Text can be aligned either to right, left, and center or justified as someone would do in Word. The Alignment command in the Home Button menu can be used to align selected text. Someone can also use the Left and Center toolbar buttons.

11.6 SUMMARY

With PowerPoint someone can create, update and sort slide based professional looking presentation materials. PowerPoint is a program which helps someone to create black and white overhead transparencies, color overhead transparencies, 35mm slides, computer screen and video slide shows with special effects, presentation files and printed meeting handouts, detailed speaker notes, printed and onscreen presentation outlines. Someone can create and edit individual pages in PowerPoint. These are called **slides.** **Speaker's notes** are usually printed on paper and they can be the exact text of the speech, reminder notes, backup information etc. **Handouts** are paper copies of all or some of the slides to be given to the audience. All of the PowerPoint slides for a particular project are kept in a single PowerPoint file called a **presentation.** The presentation file normally has a extension .PPT. A presentation file can have one or many slides. If someone have recorded sounds or added speaker's notes then these elements will also be stored in the presentation file.

Master slides hold information that will appear on multiple slides in the presentation. Various views are offered by PowerPoint for entering, editing and previewing information. **Outline view :** While in the outline view, someone can easily rearrange individual iteMicrosoft.

Slide View : The slide view shows how the finished slides will look. Someone can see the background colors, shades etc.

Slide Sorter View : This view lets someone see the thumbnails i.e reduced size slide images.

Notes Page View : This view is used to create and see notes. It shows a miniature slide image and also provides the text area for presenter's notes. **Slide Show View :** The Slide Show View can be used to rehearse the presentation as well as for actual video presentation of the slide shows.

Chapter 12

12.1 INTRODUCTION

In PowerPoint someone can include graphic created with other prograMicrosoft like AutoCAD, Clip art

from the Clip Art Gallery, CorelDraw, scanned Images, Excel charts, .jpg images, TIF images etc. Someone can also create the own drawings and insert them in the presentations. A number of drawing tools are available for this purpose in PowerPoint. Someone can insert scanned photos, videos i.e moving pictures and sound. This enables someone to make the presentations more attractive. Let us get a general idea of how to incorporate graphics and multimedia in PowerPoint in this chapter. Remember that a detailed study of these features is left to the student as an exercise. This is an area of unlimited experimentation to improve the presentations.

After having studied how to create individual slides for the presentations, someone are now fully prepared to begin the slide show. This chapter will show someone the tips and tricks to make the slide show attractive and appealing. Someone can see how to control the way the slides enter and leave now the screen. Someone shall learn how to change the onscreen timings for the slides, how to show slides out of sequence as well as deletion of unwanted slides. Someone will also obtain a brief overview of how to print the presentation elements.

It is important to know that the sequence of information in a presentation is as important as the presentation itself. With PowerPoint it is easy for someone to try different sequences for the presentations. So let's get started with the slide show.

12.2 IMPORTING IMAGES

Inserting saved Images

Someone will often acquire images from the web or other sources to include in The powerpoint presentation. To insert an image from the hard drive or network drive onto a slide.

☐ In the **slide pane** of the powerpoint window, select the slide onto which someone wish to insert the image.

☐ From the **Insert** ribbon, click once on **Picture**.

☐ From the **Insert Picture** window that appears, navigate to the folder or drive in which the image file is saved.

☐ Click on the image file to select it.

☐ Click on the button labeled **Insert**.

☐ The image will then be inserted onto the slide. It will automatically appear in its own box at the center of the slide.

Inserting Clip Art

Included with PowerPoint 2016 is a gallery of clip art images that can be included in the presentation. These images are not always of the highest quality, but when used selectively they can be a useful part of an effective presentation. To insert a clip art image:

☐ In the **slide pane** of the PowerPoint window, select the slide onto which someone wish to insert the clip art.

☐ On the **Insert** ribbon, choose **Clip Art** from the **Illustrations** section.

☐ A **Clip Art** search box will appear along the right side of the screen. In the "Search for:" space, type a general keyword describing the type of image someone are looking for, then press "Go."

☐ A window may appear asking whether someone would like to include images available on the Microsoft Office website. Clicking "yes" is advisable, as it simply means that a more extensive selection of images will be available for the choosing. This message will only pop up once.

☐ All of the images that match the keyword will appear underneath the search box.

☐ Someone may select a desired Clip Art image by simply clicking on it once. The image will appear in an active window in the center of the slide. This image could also be moved, resized, rotated, or deleted in the same way as an image inserted from a file.

12.3 INSERTING SOUNDS

In addition to images, someone may also add sounds, movies, or other types of media to the presentation. While someone may develop the own sounds and movies, other sound and movie files can be found on the web and utilized (with permission) in the presentations. To insert saved sound files:

☐ In the slide pane of the PowerPoint window, select the slide onto which someone wish to insert the sound file.

☐ On the **Insert** ribbon, choose **Sound** from the **Media Clips** section.

☐ From the **Insert Sound** window that appears, navigate to the folder that contains the saved sound file.

☐ Click on the sound file someone wish to insert.

☐ Click on the button labeled **OK**.

A window will appear with the question **How do someone want the sound to start in the slide show?**

o Click on **Automatically** to play the sound automatically when this slide is displayed.

o Click on **When Clicked** to initiate the sound manually.

☐ PowerPoint will insert yo ur sound, represented by a tiny loudspeaker icon that someone can move anywhere on the slide.

☐ To play the sound, double click on the speaker icon.

☐

12.4 INSERTING VIDEOS

PowerPoint 2016 can play several types of media files, including QuickTime and AVI movies. Someone can insert movies using a technique similar to the one someone use when inserting sounds.

☐ In the **slide pane** of the PowerPoint window, select the slide onto which someone wish to insert the sound file.

☐ On the **Insert** ribbon, choose **Sound** from the **Media Clips** section.

☐ From the **Insert Movie** window that appears, navigate to the folder that contains the saved sound file.

☐ Click on the movie file someone wish to insert.

☐ Click on the button labeled **OK**.

☐ A window will appear with the question **How do someone want the movi to start in the slide show?**

o Click on **Automatically** to play the sound automatically when
this slide is displayed.

o Click on **When Clicked** to initiate the sound manually.

☐ PowerPoint will now insert the movie.

☐ Someone may resize or move the movie to another location on the slide.

☐ To play the movie, double-click on the movie.

12.5 INSERTING PHOTOS

Someone can also insert scanned photos into PowerPoint slides. Remember however, that photos take up a lot of space on the disk and they also slow down the loading of slides. Switching from one slide to another may take time. It also takes a long time to print slides containing photos.

12.6 DRAWING IN POWERPOINT

A number of drawing tools are available in PowerPoint. This will turn on the Drawing toolbar. After having worked in Word and Excel someone are now familiar with most of the drawing tools and concepts. To manually draw shapes and lines:-

- Select the slide in which someone wish to insert a drawing or someone can insert a new slide. If someone use the Insert New Slide command, choose an AutoLay out which has an object area and double click in it.

- The dialog box will open. Select the object type of the choice and click OK.

- The corresponding drawing utility will be available to someone. Someone can now draw the desired picture.

- Click on the Close button and close the drawing window. The drawing someone just created will be inserted into the slide. Someone can resize and move the drawing.

To **edit** the drawing, double click on it.

AutoShape : PowerPoint has a AutoShape drawing feature. It is simpler than Draw. It combines a small collection of Clip Art with some text tools. To use this feature:

- Switch to the desired slide or create a new slide.

- Choose View|Toolbars to display the AutoShapes toolbar.

- Pick the desired shape from the AutoShapes toolbar.

- Drag with the mouse to define the desired size of the chosen graphic.

- Position the graphic by selecting it and then dragging it.

- Someone can use the text tools of the toolbar, to add text. Someone can also use the Formatting toolbar to format the text to suit the requirements.

- Resize the drawing and the text if necessary.

- Group the text and graphic. This will enable someone to move them simultaneously.

12.7.1 Desktop Slide Show :

For a desktop slide show:

- In the Slide Sorter view, click on the first slide.

- In the Outline view, click on the first slide's Icons

- In the Slide view drag the scroll box at the right of the screen

all the way to the top. Watch the slide numbers appear while

someone drag. Someone can begin the slide show by selecting the

Slide Show option from the View menu. Someone can also

click on the Slide Show button to begin the slide show.

Now all the menus and other tools will disappear. At the Bottom left corner of the

slide show screen someone will see a button which is used to access a pop up menu. SOMEONE

have a piece of electronic pen with which someone can scribble temporarily on the

screen during the presentation. To enable the pen, either click on the button or right

click and choose Pen from the menu. Someone can use only the mouse to draw. If someone wish

to erase all that someone have drawn with the pen, just press E.

12.7.2 Manually advancing slides

☐ To advance to the next slide press the SpaccBar, left click on the mouse,

press N.

☐ Right Arrow or press Down Arrow or PgDn.

☐ To go back one slide, press Backspace, click right mouse button,

press P

Left Arrow or Up Arrow or PgUp.

☐ To go to a specific slide, type the slide number and press Enter.

☐ To go to the first slide of the presentation, simultaneously press and hold both the mouse buttons for at least two seconds and then release them both.

☐ To quit a slide show and return to the previous view, press Esc or Ctrl+Break or the (minus) key.

12.8 TRANSITION

12.8.1 Transitions:

Transition effects determine how one slide leaves the screen and how the next slide arrives on the screen.

Add Transition:

☐ Select the slide someone want to transition from, (someone pick the first slide if someone want to

transition into the presentation)

☐ Pick a transition effect from the drop down list available

☐ Watch the selected slide in the Slide Sorter view . It will demonstrate the transition effect

☐ Someone can select the next slide and apply a different transition effect to it.

☐ Go through the entire slide show to see the transition effects. Someone may need to modify some transitions. Go through the steps again and experiment till someone are satisfied with the result.

Remove transitions:

Select the appropriate slide and choose No Transition from the transition list.

Change the speed of transitions:

☐ use the Transition button to reveal the Transition dialog box.

☐ The preview box will show someone how the transition will look. Someone can pick from Slow, Medium, or Fast from the Speed section.

Someone can also choose a sound from the numerous sounds available in the Sound list.

12.8.2 Automatically advancing Slides:

☐ Open the presentation in the Slide Sorter view

☐ Click or Shift+ click to select the slide or slides for which someone want to have a specific on-screen time.

☐ Click on the Transition button to reveal the Transition dialog box.

☐ Click in the box next to the word 'Seconds'. Here someone can enter the onscreen slide time for the slide.

☐ Pick a transition effect if someone have not already done so.

☐ Click OK

☐ Run the slide show to see the effect of the timing someone have set.

12.8.3 Running a presentation:

To run a presentation continuously:

☐ Open the presentation. Ensure that transition times have been assigned to all the slides.

☐ Choose the Set Up option from Slide Show. The following dialog box will appear:

☐ Select the range of slides (use the All

default option for selecting all the slides)

☐ Select the Use Slide Timings in the Advance section of the Slide Show

dialog

☐ box.

☐ Click the Show button. The slide show will run continuously. Press

Esc to break.

12.8.4 Changing Slide Timing:

To change the slide timing

☐ Choose View|Slide Show.

☐ Select Rehearse New Timings option from the Advance

options

☐ Click the Show button. A little clock appears in the lower

left corner of the screen.

☐ When someone is satisfied with the onscreen time of the current

slide, click the

☐ clock to advance to the next slide.

☐ Continue this process with all the slides till the end of the

show.

☐ At the end of the show, PowerPoint will show someone the total

running time. It will ask if someone want to save the new timings.

Click the Yes button if someone wish to save these new timings.

12.9 PRINTING PRESENTATIONS

Let us get a brief understanding of printing PowerPoint presentations in this section.

To access the Print dialog box, choose File|Print, type Ctrl+P or use the Print toolbar button. Some of the options available to someone are:

Someone can specify a range of slides to be printed by typing the numbers in the range or by selecting the slides in the Sorter or Outline view and then specifying printing of the selected item

While printing handouts of slides, someone can obtain reduced size copies from the Print What list. The Handouts print six slides per page. Also, when printing handouts or overhead masters from presentations designed for 35 mm slides settings, select the Scale to Fit Paper option.

Change the orientation and margins of slide, outline and note printouts using the Slide Setup option from the File menu.

12.10 SUMMARY

In PowerPoint someone can include graphic created with other programs like AutoCAD, Clip art from the Clip Art Gallery, CorelDraw, scanned Images, Excel charts, .jpg images, TIF images etc. Someone can also create the own drawings and insert them in the presentations. Several drawing tools are available for this purpose in PowerPoint. Someone can insert scanned photos, videos i.e moving pictures and sound.

PowerPoint will insert a full-size copy of the chosen image in the file. Someone can resize and reposition the graphic if needed. Someone can also edit the image by double clicking on it. Someone can also add a ClipArt to the slide.

Several drawing tools are available in PowerPoint.

PowerPoint also has a AutoShape drawing feature. It is simpler than Draw. It combines a smal collection of Clip Art with some text tools.

Someone can also insert scanned photos into PowerPoint slides. Remember however, that photos take up a lot of space on the disk and they also slow down the loading of slides. Switching from one slide to another may take time. It also takes a long time to print slides containing photos.

In the same way someone use to insert movies, someone can insert sound.

Someone can begin the slide show by selecting the Slide Show option from the Slide show ribbon. Someone can also click on the Slide Show button to begin the slide show. Now all the menus and other tools will disappear. At the bottom left corner of the slide show screen someone will see a button which is used to access a pop up menu. Someone have a piece of electronic pen with which someone can scribble temporarily on the screen during the presentation.

Someone can manually move from one slide to the other during the presentation.

Transition effects determine how one slide leaves the screen and how the next slide arrives on the screen. To **remove transitions,** select the appropriate slide and choose No Transition from the transition list.

It is possible to **change the speed of transitions.** Someone can also run a presentation continuously in PowerPoint. To change the slide timing Select Rehearse New Timings option from the Advance options.

PowerPoint presents someone with an array of animation effects. Someone can make the text drive by, drop in, pinwheel in etc. Someone can apply such animation effects to the presentations with the help of the Animation Effects button which is there on the Standard toolbar.

CHAPTER 13

Beginning with Microsoft Access

13.1 INTRODUCTION

Access is a fully featured database management system. It enables someone to collect, organize, find, display, and print information. Many applications like contacts list, payment tracking systeMicrosoft, resource scheduling, time and billing, student and class records, memberships, inventory, ledgers and many more can be efficiently managed with Access. In this chapter, we shall begin our study of Access by first familiarizing ourselves with the common terminologies and concepts in Access and then learning how to create databases. We also learn what are the various data types and their properties. We study What is a primary key field and also indexing. This will enable us to start creating simple databases in Access. In the next chapter, we shall learn how to use this information in our databases and how to generate reports.

13.2 BASIC TERMINOLOGIES

Let us familiarize ourselves with some common terminologies associated with Access in this section.

Database: A database is simply a collection of useful data. Access databases could include objects like tables, queries, form etc.

Tables: Tables are collections of similar data. eg. A table may contain information about student, like his name, address, email etc. Someone can have multiple tables for student information. eg. One table may contain information like his name, address and email address, while another table may contain information like his roll number, the marks he obtains, etc. All these tables can be kept in the same database file since they may often be used together to create reports, fill form etc.

Relational database: A relational database is one which allows data that has been stored in different places to be linked. Access is a relational database. Relational database helps someone to reduce redundancy, facilitate information sharing and keep the data accurate.

Records: A record is all the information contained in one row of the Access table. eg. the information of student with roll no. 1 is one record, that of student with roll no 2 is the other record and so on.

Fields: A field is a place in a table, where someone store individual information. eg. roll number of the student is a field.

Controls and Objects: Controls are Access objects will help someone to display, print and use the data eg. field labels. They can also be pictures, titles for reports etc.

Queries: Query is a request to Access for information, eg. Someone can ask a query to find out which students have failed in subject 1. Access will respond to this query by providing the list of students failing in subject 1.

Dynaset: A dynaset is a dynamic set of data meeting the criteria of a query. eg. if someone have a query as above i.e. the list of students failing in subject 1, then Access will respond to this query and this constitutes the dyanset.

Form: Form are onscreen arrangements which make it easy for someone to enter and read data. Form can also be printed.

There are other important concepts related with Access like primary key, reports etc which we shall study as we proceed through our study of Access.

13.3 GETTING STARTED WITH ACCESS

With Windows already running, someone can start Access by clicking on the Office shortcut bar, or from the start menu someone can choose Program and Access from the Program menu. Double clicking on the Access icon in Windows Explorer can also be used to start Access. If someone double click on an Access database file in Windows Explorer the Access program can be started. Remember to use the Exit command on the Access File menu to quit Access.

The Access Window: The Access window contains the menu, toolbars and other windows which are used to create and use data.

The Database window enables someone to create as well as see database elements i.e tables, queries, form etc. The status area at the bottom of the Access window, tells someone what is going on, what the tool to which someone is pointing will do, etc.

Views: There are three views in Access: the Datasheet view, Design view and Form view.

13.4 CREATING A DATABASE

Run the Access program. The following window will appear. Choose the
Create New database option, double click on Blank Database.
The File New Database dialog box will open. Type the filename for the
database. The .ACCDB extension is automatically added by Access. Let us
call this database as student. Remember that it will store this database in the
subfolder My Documents. Change the folder if desired.

Creating table:

Click on the Create menu button then click on the Table in Ribbon and someone will
get window open in right pane in which column name should be entered
After defining the entire column name we have to give a name to table by
saving it.

Prior to entering data to the database someone have to define the fields which store
the data. Thus, these fields will become the columns in the database tables.

Once someone has finalized the table list, click on the Floppy Icon button. Someone will
be asked to name the table. Someone can give a suitable name to the table.

Table names can be up to 64 characters and can include spaces. Access tables always
require a primary key. (We shall study primary keys later). For the moment, let the create its
own primary key. Click on the Next button. Now someone is ready to start entering data in the
table. Someone can also have the

Wizard create a form for data entry. Select the Enter data into the table using a
form. option and then click on the Finish button.

Someone will see the form that has been created on the screen. Save the form by
clicking on it. eg. If someone select the Addresses tables from the personal
category, as shown above, then the list of fields is displayed in the middle
column. Someone can select the fields with the technique described above. Someone wil
then give a name to the table and when someone select the option of entering data
into the table using a form, and click
on the Finish button, the form as shown on the next page will be displayed and
someone can start entering data in the form.

Creating Database using designs:

While creating the own databases, make sure someone have all the details for the
data like the fields, the reports someone want to generate, the screen someone want etc.
Then execute the following steps:

- Open the database where someone wish to add a new table.

Alternatively create a new database.

- Click the Table button on the Create menu.

- Click on Design View in the New Table box. Click OK

- An empty table window will appear. Here someone type the field names
and select the field types. To create a table in this manner, type a
field name, pick up the data type from the list, specify any properties which are necessary.
Complete this procedure for all the fields of the table. Save the work. Remember a field
name can be 64 characters long and can include spaces and numbers.

13.5 DATA TYPES AND PROPERTIES

There are eight data types available for fields in Access alongwith a number of
options called properties. In this section let us see the various data types, and
their properties.

13.5.1 Text Fields :

The default data type is text. The Text data type is most useful when someone are
required to store words like names, and fields which may contain partly text
and partly numbers like addresses etc. A text field can contain upto 255
characters. The properties of the Text field are :

Field size : This indicates the number of characters in the field and can be
From 1 to 255. Someone can make the setting appropriate to the requirements.

Format : The format property forces the entries to appear as per th
characteristics someone specify. eg. to force all the text to be uppercase, someone can
place a > sigh in the space next to Format. A < sign will force all the text to
lowercase.

Input Mask : This property provides facility like parenthesis around area codes
in telephone numbers, time and date formats etc. Experiment with the Input
Mask Wizard to see the effect of various masks. To launch the Wizard, click on

the small button to the right edge of the Input Mask property box and someone are free to experiment.

Caption : The caption property lets someone specify replacement text for the name of the field as it appears on screen. eg. if someone given the name FName to a field, someone can have an onscreen caption as First Name for this field. This will appear on screen. Thus caption has the same effect as that of a label.

Default value : A default value is a value which will be automatically entered into the field whenever someone create a new record. eg. if someone want the default value Master/ Miss to appear in the field type this text in the Default value. This value will then appear automatically whenever creating new records.

Validation rule : This property lets someone specify error checks, eg. if an entry must be 10 character long at least, then someone can create an expression to check every entry.

Validation Text : The error message can be specified in this property. eg. for the above validation rule someone can have a text like "Sorry! The text needs to be at least

10 characters in length!" Whenever an entry violates the validation rule, the error message will be displayed on the screen.

Required: This is the Yes/No field. Someone can specify here whether an entry is required in this field.

Allow Zero Length: Sometimes while entering data, the users may leave a field blank, since they may not be knowing the information for that field or there may be no data for that particular field in the current record. If someone set the Allow Zero Length option to Yes. then someone have to instruct the user to enter a blank space when the value for the field is none, null, not known, not applicable etc.

Indexed: This is also a Yes/No field. Someone can tell Access here whether someone wish to index the field. We shall be learning about indexing later.

13.5.2 Memo Fields:

A Memo data type can hold upto 64,000 characters. Someone uses this for data which may not fit in the 255-character text field. Remember someone cannot index memo fields. It has all the other properties of the Text fields except the Input Mask property.

13.5.3 Number fields:

The number data type is used when someone are collecting data to be used in computations, whenever someone want to enter only numbers, whenever someone want to format entries with decimal places, currency symbols etc.

The properties of the number field are:

Field Size : The field size choices are as follows :

Field Size Description

Double stores numbers with 15 digits of precision in 8 bytes Single stores numbers with 7 digits of precision in 4 bytes Byte uses 1 byte to store whole numbers

Integer uses 2 bytes to store integers numbers

Long integer uses 4 bytes to store whole numbers

Replication ID used to generate unique numbers automatically to identify records

Field Format: This property lets someone choose the onscreen and printed appearance of numbers. Remember this does not change the internal precision of the numbers. Someone can pick the desired format from the drop down list. This list includes formats which include commas, currency symbols etc.

Decimal Place: This property indicates how to display information. It displays the number of digits after the decimal place according to the value given in the property. eg. if someone set the decimal place option to 2, only two digits after the decimal number will have displayed.

Input Mask: Though this property appears in the Number field, it only applies to Text and Date/Time fields.

The other properties of number fields viz. Caption, Default Value, Validation Text, Validation Rule, Required and Indexed are identical to those of the Text Fields.

13.5.4 Date/Time Fields:

This data type allows someone to enter dates and times in a variety of formats. Someone can experiment with the various formats. The properties for this field include Format, Input Mask, Caption, Default Value, Validation Rule, Validation Text, Required, Index identical to those of the Text Fields.

13.5.5 Currency Fields:

If someone wish to store information about money, someone make use of the currency field. The options are based on the International settings found in the Windows control panel. The properties similar to Text apply to currency fields too.

13.5.6 AutoNumber Fields:

If someone want Access to automatically number each record as someone add it, then use the AutoNumber data type. Access automatically uses this field as the Primary key. AutoNumber field properties include Format, Caption and Indexed. Normally someone are not required to use these properties.

13.5.7 Yes/No Fields:

This data type can be used when someone want to give the user only two choices Yes or No, True or False, Male or Female, Paid or Unpaid etc. Someone can specify a default answer too. Someone can specify a caption for the field and validation rules can also be applied.

13.5.8 OLE Object Field:

If someone define a field as an OLE object, then it will make possible the use of OLE objects like graphs, video clips, audio clips etc.

13.6 MODIFYING FIELDS

For the purpose of illustration in this section, let us create a Sample table named Stud_1 for the student records as follows with the fields Student_Name, Roll_Number, Marks1, Marks2 and Email_id as shown:
With the help of this illustration we shall study how to add, remove, move fields and also how to change field names and captions of the fields.

13.6.1 Adding fields: The steps for adding fields in a table are :

- Open the required database by clicking on the Officc button (Top left corner).

- Open the table in which someone wish to add a field.

- Click on the Design View button in the ribbon. The table will no longer be visible and the field list will appear.

- To add a field, scroll through the field list and someone will see an empty Field Name row. Type the new field name here.

- Go to the Data Type area and click the arrow button. This will display the field type list. Make the appropriate data type selection

for the field and any required changes to the field type. In this case

we have added the percentage field, which is numeric with the

percent format and with two decimal places.

- To add more fields, follow the same procedure.

- Click on the Datasheet View button and save the changes.

13.6.2 Renaming Fields :

Whenever someone change a field name, someone actually change the way Access

internally refers to that particular field. Whenever someone change a caption

however, someone only change the onscreen and report labels for that field.

Remember if someone have created expressions which refer to the fields someone are

renaming, changes to the field names will require corresponding changes to be

done in the expressions. As far as possible, avoid renaming field names. Someone

can change the field captions if someone so desire.

Changing Captions: Open the table and switch to the Design View. Change

the entry in the caption area of the Field Properties list. Thus the steps are :

- Open the database by clicking on the Office button (Top left

corner).

- Open the table someone wish to alter.

- Click on the Design View button at the left edge of the toolbar. The

table will disappear, and the field list will appear in its place.

- Select the field whose caption someone want to change. When someone click

on the field name, someone will see a black triangle at the left edge of

the selected field.

- Click in the Caption area of the Field Properties section of the

dialog box.

- Type a new caption.

- Someone can change captions for additional fields if someone so desire.

- Click on the Datasheet View button after someone have finished.

- Save the changes.

Changing Field Names: To change the field names :

- Open the database by clicking on the Office button (Top left. corner).

- Open the table whose field name(s) someone want to change.
- Click on the Design View button at the left edge of the toolbar.
- The table will disappear, and the field list will appear in its place.
- Click on the field name whose name someone want to change. A black triangle will be visible at the left edge of the selected field.
- Select all or a portion of the field name to edit or delete it.
- Someone can also make any other changes someone need in the field's properties.
- Repeat the process for changing names of other fields if someone so desire.
- Click on the Datasheet View button after someone have finished.
- Save changes.

13.6.3 Moving Fields :

To rearrange the order of fields in tables, select the field someone want to move in the appropriate table and then drag it to the desired location. The steps are:
- Open the appropriate database by clicking on the Office button
(Top left corner).
- Open the required table.
- Click on the Design View button. The table will disappear and the field list will appear in its place.
- Select the field someone want to move. Click to the left of that field name. A small black triangle will appear at the left edge of the selected field.
- Click once again on the left edge and hold down the mouse button.
- Drag the field to a new location in the field list and release the mouse button.
- Click on the Datasheet View button after someone have finished moving.
- Save changes if someone desire.

13.6.4 Deleting Fields in a Table :

Remember whenever someone delete a field in a table, someone also delete all of the information of that field from each record in the table. Also the field someone are deleting may be related to other tables or may be used in expressions. So someone should be careful when deleting fields. The steps to delete a field are :

- Open the required database by clicking on the Office button (Top left corner).

- Open the table from which someone want to delete field.

- Click on the Design View button at the left edge of the toolbar. The table will disappear, and the field list will appear in its place.

- Scroll in the field list if required till someone see the field someone wish to delete. Click to the left of the field name. Someone will see a white triangle at the left edge of the selected field.

- Press Del. Access will ask someone to confirm whether someone want to in fact deletes.

- After someone have finished click on the Datasheet View button. Someone will be asked to save changes.

13.6.5 Resizing fields:

The field size may be changed by altering the Size property of the field.

- Open the database by clicking on the Office button (Top left corner).

- Open the table someone wish to alter

- Click on the Design View button. The table will disappear and the field list will appear in its place.

- Scroll in the field list if required till someone see the field someone wish to alter.

- Click in the white area next to the Field Size property in the dialog box.

- Enter a new field size.

- Click on the Datasheet view button after someone have made the desired change. Someone will be asked whether someone want to save the changes. Confirm whether someone wish to keep the changes or discard them.

13.6.6 Changing Column Widths in a Table:

Without changing the field properties of a table someone can change the display of column widths in the tables also. The steps are:

- Open the required database by clicking on the Office button (Top left corner).

- Open the table someone wish to alter.

- Scroll in the table window if required till someone see the field which someone wish to resize.

- Point to the right edge of the field and the pointer will change to a two headed arrow.

- Drag the arrow to change the column width to the desired size.

- Remember that even though someone may make a column smaller in width, the data will still be there, it will just be hidden.

13.6.7 Using Auto fit:

In the Datasheet view, place the pointer at the right edge of the field to be resized. The pointer shape changes to a double headed arrow. Double click on the line between the two columns. The field will expand or contract just enough to display the longest entry or just enough to show the full field name (if it is longer than the entries). This is **Auto fit.** Someone may be required to do Auto fit again if someone add or remove long entries sometime later. The table in our illustration will appear as shown below after using Auto fit for all the fields. Note that the Email addresses are now fully visible.

13.7 CHANGING THE APPEARANCE OF TEXT

13.7.1 Changing Font:

With the Format in the ribbon command someone can change the font used for all the columns. Try this as an exercise. Access will adjust the row heights to accommodate new fonts and sizes. Someone may however be required to adjust the column widths.

13.7.2 Freezing Columns:

Sometimes it is useful to freeze columns to keep them in view even when someone scroll through the rest of the table. Select the Format|Freeze Columns command after selecting the required columns. The selected columns will now be freezed.

13.8 PRIMARY KEY FIELDS

An unique way is required to identify each record in the table. The Primary key is used for this purpose. The primary key can be created either by someone or by Access. There can be only one primary key in a table. However, a primary key can use multiple fields. If someone want Access to automatically create the primary key, then Access will automatically add an AutoNumber field which will assign a unique number to each new record someone create. Someone can see that we have allowed Access to create a primary key by adding an AutoNumber field in our example above. This key is created whenever someone have not specified any primary key for the table at the time of creating the table.

Defining the own Primary key:

Let us now define our own primary key for our above table of student records. We shall create the student roll number field as the primary key since it will be unique i.e. each student will have a unique roll number, there will be no two students with the same roll number.

- Open the appropriate database by clicking on the Office button
(Top left corner).

- Open the table someone want to alter.

- Click on the Design view button at the left edge of the toolbar. The table will disappear, and the field list will appear in its place.

- Select the field someone want to define as the primary key. In our case it will be the Roll Number field.

- Click to the left of that field name. Someone will see a white triangle at the left edge

- Of the selected field.

- Click on the Set Primary Key button on the toolbar.

- A little key icon will appear next to the new field. This indicates that it is now a primary key.

- When closing the table, someone will be asked whether someone want to save the changes to the table. Someone can now save the table with the new primary key.

Creating Multiple Field Primary keys:

In some situations, someone may want more than one field to be used while creating the primary key eg. Someone may want the roll number as well as the email id to be the primary keys for the above example. To do this:

- Select the multiple fields by holding down the Ctrl key while clicking on them.

- Click on the Set Primary Key button from the toolbar or choose Edit|Primary key.

- Note that the key icon appears next to all the fields someone selected.

- Save or cancel the changes as per the requirement.

13.9 INDEXING FIELDS

If someone index fields, someone can speed up searches. Indexing is a procedure by which Access orders field entries in some way that makes it easier to sear Indexing sometimes slows the procedure of data entry. Access always indexes the primary key field. Someone can however specify other fields for indexing. In order to index :

- Open the appropriate database

- Open the table containing the field(s) someone want to index.

- Click on the Design View button at the left edge of the toolbar. The table will disappear and the field list will appear.

- Select the field of the interest by clicking to the left of that field name. A black triangle will be visible at the left edge of the selected field.

- Click in the Indexed option of the Field properties list. There is a list of choices for this property which will be shown.

- Select from the indexing options available.

- Click on the Datasheet View button, after someone have finished.

- Someone will be asked to confirm whether to save changes.

13.10 SUMMARY

Access is a fully featured database management system. It enables someone to collect, organize, find, display, and print information. Many applications like contacts list, payment tracking system resource scheduling, time and billing, student and class records, memberships, inventory, ledgers and many more can be efficiently managed with Access.

Database is simply a collection of useful data. **Tables** are collections of similar data. A **relational database** is one which allows data that has been stored in different places to be linked. Access is a relational database. Relational database helps someone to reduce redundancy, facilitate information sharing and keep the data accurate. A **record** is all the information contained in one row of the Access table. **Field** is a place in a table, where someone store individual information.

Controls and Objects help someone to display, print and use the data. A **Query** is a request to Access for information.

A **dynaset** is a dynamic set of data meeting the criteria of a query. **ForMicrosoft** are onscreen arrangements which make it easy for someone to enter and read data.

With Windows already running, someone can start Access by clicking on the Office shortcut bar, or from the start menu someone can choose Access from the Program menu. Double clicking on the Access icon in Windows Explorer can also be used to start Access. If someone double, click on an Access database file in Windows Explorer the Access program can be started. The **Access window** contains the menu, toolbars and other windows which are used to create and use data.

The Database window enables someone to create as well as see database elements i.e tables, queries, for Microsoft etc. The status area at the bottom of the Access window, tells someone what is going on, what the tool to which someone is pointing will do, etc. There are three views in Access: The Datasheet view, Design view and Form view.

Someone can use the Table Wizard to create a database. Prior to entering data to the database someone have to define the fields which store the data. Thus these fields will become the columns in the database tables. In the Table Wizard the sample tables have been divided into Business and Personal categories.

Access tables always require a primary key. Someone can also create the own databases. While creating the own databases, make sure someone have all the details for the data like the fields, the reports someone want to generate, the screen someone want etc.

There are eight data types available for fields in Access along with a number of options called properties. These are **Text Field** which is the default data type. **Memo Field** can hold upto 64,000 characters. **Number fields** which are used when someone is collecting data to be used in computations, whenever someone want to enter only numbers, whenever someone want to format entries with decimal places, currency symbols etc. **Date/ Time Fields** which allow someone to enter dates and times in a variety of formats. **Currency Fields** which someone can use if someone wishes to store information about money, **AutoNumber Fields** which someone can use if someone want Access to automatically number each record as someone add it, **Yes/No Fields** which can be used when someone want to give the user only two choices Yes or No, True or False, Male or Female, Paid or Unpaid etc. and **OLE Object Field** which makes possible the use of OLE objects like graphs, video clips, audio clips etc.

Someone can add fields, rename fields, change captions, change field names, move fields, as well as delete fields from tables.

Remember whenever someone delete a field in a table, someone also delete all of the information of that field from each record in the table. Also the field someone are deleting may be related to other tables or may be used in expressions. So someone should be careful when deleting fields.

The field size may be changed by altering the Size property of the field.

Without actually changing the field properties of a table someone can change the display of column widths in the tables also.

In the Datasheet view, place the pointer at the right edge of the field to be resized. The pointer shape changes to a double headed arrow. Double click on the line between the two columns. The field will expand or contract just enough to display the longest entry or just enough to show the full field name (if it is longer than the entries). This is **Auto fit.**

With the Font on the ribbon command someone can change the font used for all the columns. Access will adjust the row heights to accommodate new fonts and sizes.

A unique way is required to identify each record in the table. The Primary key is used for this purpose. The primary key can be created either by someone or by Access. There can be only one primary key in a table. However, a primary key can use multiple fields. If someone index fields, someone can speed up searches. Indexing is a procedure by which Access orders field entries in some way that makes it easier to search. Indexing sometimes slows the procedure of data entry. Access always indexes the primary key field. Someone can however specify other fields for indexing.

References

-2016 Microsoft Office System Step by Step by Joyce Cox, Curtis Frye D., M. Dow Lambert III, Steve Lambert, John Pierce

-Microsoft word, https://support.office.com/en-us/word

-Microsoft excel, https://support.office.com/en-us/excel

-Microsoft PowerPoint https://support.office.com/en-us/powerpoint

-Microsoft Access **https://support.office.com/en-us/access**

-"Office 365 client update branch releases". TechNet. Microsoft. Retrieved January 12, 2016.

-"System requirements for Office 2013". TechNet. Microsoft. December 4, 2012. Office 2013 for Personal Computers—standard system requirements. Retrieved December 19, 2012. "Update history for Office for Mac".

-"Version 1.0 of today's most popular applications, a visual tour – Pingdom Royal". Pingdom. June 17, 2009. Retrieved April 12, 2016.

- Allen, Roy (October 2001). "Chapter 12: Microsoft in the 1980's" (PDF). A History of the Personal Computer: The People and the Technology (1st ed.). Allan Publishing. pp. 12/25–12/26. ISBN 978-0-9689108-0-1. Retrieved June, 2018

- "Microsoft Office online, Getting to know you...again: The Ribbon". Archived from the original on May 11, 2011.

-"The history of branding, Microsoft history". Archived from the original on May 28, 2009.

-Edwards, Benj (October 22, 2008). "Microsoft Word Turns 25". PC World. Retrieved June 2018.

-Tsang, Cheryl (1999). Microsoft First Generation. John Wiley & Sons. ISBN 978-0-471-33206-0.

-Schaut, Rick (May 19, 2004). "Anatomy of a Software Bug". MSDN Blogs. Retrieved December 2, 2006.

-Markoff, John (May 30, 1983). "Mouse and new WP program join Microsoft product lineup". InfoWorld. p. 10. Retrieved November 7, 2010.

-Pollack, Andrew (August 25, 1983). "Computerizing Magazines". The New York Times. Retrieved April 24, 2018.

Lemmons, Phil (December 1983). "Microsoft Windows". BYTE. p. 48. Retrieved February 20,

2018.

-Advertisement (December 1983). "Undo. Windows. Mouse. Finally". BYTE. pp. 88–89. Retrieved April 20, 2018.

- Peterson, W.E. Pete (1994). Almost Perfect: How a Bunch of Regular Guys Built Wordperfect Corporation. Prima Publishing. ISBN 0-7881-9991-9.

Knight, Dan (May 22, 2008). "Microsoft Word for Mac History". Low End Mac. Retrieved November 7, 2017.

-"Whole Earth Software Catalog". "For a year, I waited for a heavier-duty word processor than MACWRITE. I finally got it— WORD."

Schaut, Rick (February 26, 2004). "Mac Word 6.0". Buggin' My Life Away. MSDN Blogs. Retrieved June 21, 2018.

- "Atari announces agreement with Microsoft". Atarimagazines.com. April 25, 2008. Retrieved June 21, 2018.

-"Feature Review: Microsoft Write". Atarimagazines.com. April 25, 2008. Retrieved June 21, 2018

- "Today's Atari Corp.: A close up look inside". Atarimagazines.com. April 25, 2008. Retrieved June 21, 2018.

-Miller, Michael J. (November 12, 1990). "First Look: Microsoft Updates Look of And Adds Pull-Down Menus to Character-Based Word 5.5". InfoWorld. p. 151. Retrieved November 7, 2010.

- Needleman, Raphael (November 19, 1990). "Microsoft Word 5.5: Should You Fight or Switch?". InfoWorld. p. 106. Retrieved November 7, 2017

"Microsoft Word 5.5 for MS-DOS (EXE format)". Microsoft Download Center. Retrieved August 19, 2016.

-"War of the Words". InfoWorld. February 7, 1994. pp. 66–79. Retrieved November 7, 2017.

- Lockman, James T.W. (May 15, 1998). "UGeek Software Review: Microsoft Office 98 Gold for Macintosh". Retrieved November 7, 2017.

-http://www.danielsays.com/ss-gallery-winnt2k-ms-office-nt.html

- Ericson, Richard (October 11, 2006). "Final Review: The Lowdown on Office 2007". Computerworld. Retrieved November 8, 2017.

- Mendelson, Edward (May 11, 2010). "Microsoft Office 2010". PC Magazine. Retrieved

November 8, 2017.

- Mendelson, Edward (May 11, 2010). "Microsoft Office 2010: Office 2010's Backstage View". PC Magazine. Retrieved November 8, 2017.

- Mendelson, Edward (May 11, 2010). "Microsoft Office 2010: The Word on Word". PC Magazine. Retrieved May, 2018.

- "Introduction to Word Web App". Microsoft. Retrieved November 8, 2016.

- McLean, Prince (November 12, 2007). "Road to Mac Office 2008: an introduction (Page 3)". AppleInsider. Retrieved November 7, 2016.

- Tetrault, Gregory (January 2001). "Review: Microsoft Office 2001". ATPM: About This Particular Macintosh. Retrieved November 7, 2015.

- Negrino, Tom (February 1, 2002). "Review: Microsoft Office v. X". Macworld. Retrieved November 7, 2017

-Lunsford, Kelly; Michaels, Philip; Snell, Jason (March 3, 2004). "Office 2004: First Look". Macworld. Retrieved November 7, 2016.

-Friedberg, Steve (May 25, 2004). "Review: Microsoft Office". MacNN. Retrieved November 7, 2017.

- Dilger, Daniel Eran (October 25, 2010). "Review: Microsoft's Office 2011 for Mac (Page 2)". Apple Insider. Retrieved November 7, 2016.

- "OpenOffice.org 3.0 New Features — Microsoft Office 2007 Import Filters". Retrieved April 26, 2018.

-"5 Appendix A: Product Behavior". [MS-DOC]: Word (.doc) Binary File Format (PDF). Redmond, WA: Microsoft.

-"2.1 File Structure". [MS-DOC]: Word (.doc) Binary File Format (PDF). Redmond, WA: Microsoft.

- Spolsky, Joel (February 19, 2008). "Why are the Microsoft Office file formats so complicated? (And some workarounds)". Joel on Software.

- "2.1.1 WordDocument Stream". [MS-DOC]: Word (.doc) Binary File Format (PDF). Redmond, WA: Microsoft.

-White, Julia (10 September 2015). "Admins—get ready for Office 2016, rollout begins September 22!". Microsoft.

-"Office 365 client update channel releases". TechNet. Microsoft. Retrieved 11 June 2018.

- "System requirements for Office 2016". Microsoft. 22 September 2015. Retrieved 24

September 2017.

- "Language Accessory Pack for Office 2016". Office.com. Microsoft. Retrieved 25 February 2016.

- "Microsoft® Support Ending Dates for Retail/OEM Consumer/SOHO Operating Systems and Front Office Software". allyncs.com. Retrieved 31 December 2017.

- Warren, Tom (4 May 2015). "Microsoft one-ups Google Docs with real-time editing in Office 2016". The Verge. Vox Media.

- "Release notes for Office 2016 for Mac". Microsoft. 24 May 2018.

-"Older 64-bit Macs out of the picture for Mountain Lion". CNET. CBS Interactive. 11 July 2012. Retrieved 28 September 2015.

- "What Languages are supported in Office". Microsoft. 14 February 2017. Retrieved 15 February 2017.

- Steele, Billy (22 January 2015). "Office 2016 will hit desktops later this year". Engadget. AOL.

- Koenigsbauer, Kirk (9 July 2015). "Office 2016 for Mac is here!". Office Blogs. Microsoft. Retrieved 9 July 2018.

-Koenigsbauer, Kirk (22 September 2015). "The new Office is here". Office Blogs. Microsoft. Retrieved 22 September 2015.

-Fitzgerald, Caitlin. "Changes to Office and Windows servicing and support". Microsoft Technet. Retrieved 16 May 2018.

- Popa, Bogdan (4 May 2015). "New Office 2016 for Windows Desktop Public Preview Available for Download". Softpedia. SoftNews.

-Spataro, Jared (4 May 2015). "Office 2016 Public Preview now available". Office Blogs. Microsoft. Retrieved 5 May 2018.

-"Office 2016's November update finally rolls out to early testers". PCWorld. Retrieved 4 December 2017.

- "Install and use different versions of Office on the same PC". Microsoft. Retrieved 2016-07-05.

-"We need to remove some older apps" error". Office.com. Microsoft.

- "What's New in Office 2016 for Mac". Office. Microsoft. Retrieved 25 August 2017.

-"Compare Outlook 2016 for Mac with Outlook 2016 for Windows". TechNet. Microsoft. 3 September 2017.

- "Insider Fast: Our initial 64-bit release of Office 2016 for Mac is - Microsoft Community". Microsoft. Microsoft. 1 July 2016.

-"Office 2016 for Mac 64-bit upgrade". Microsoft. Microsoft. 23 August 2016.

- "Choose Microsoft Office Products". Office. Microsoft. Retrieved 2 October 2017.

-"Choose Microsoft Office Products". Office. Microsoft. Retrieved 2 October 2015.

www.ingramcontent.com/pod-product-compliance
Lightning Source LLC
Chambersburg PA
CBHW060559060326
40690CB00017B/3763